# Terns *of* North America

A PHOTOGRAPHIC GUIDE

# Terns *of* North America

## A PHOTOGRAPHIC GUIDE

Cameron Cox

Princeton University Press

Princeton and Oxford

## DEDICATION

For Allison – Always my favorite.

## ACKNOWLEDGMENTS

My love of terns and, more broadly, of bird identification puzzles has been deeply influenced by time spent in the field and conversations with a number of people who have taught me valuable lessons, improved my process, and sparked my curiosity. I am grateful to all of them. Brian Ahern, Allison Anholt, George Armistead, Jim Arterburn, Shaun Bamford, Keith Barnes, Jessie Barry, Gian Basili, Ken Behrens, Carlos Bethancourt, Gavin Bieber, Wes Biggs, Stephanie Bilodeau, Jeff Bouton, Bill Boyle, Michael Brothers, Chris Brown, Jen Brumfield, Tamie Bulow, Iain Campbell, Phil Chaon, Scarlet Colley, Mike Crewe, Richard Crossley, Jim Danzenbaker, Ian Davies, Glen and Kashi Davis, Pablo Cervantes Daza, Jon Dunn, Pete Dunne, Gail Dwyer, Charlie Fisher, Ted Floyd, Bob Fogg, Tom Ford-Hutchinson, Dave Gagne, Emily Heiser Galick, Sam Galick, Richard Gibbons, Doug Gochfeld, Dave Goodwin, John Groskopf, Paul and Anita Guris, Skye Haas , Matt Hafner, Chris Hajduk, Brandon Holden, Marshal Iliff, João Jara, Alvaro Jaramillo, Tom Johnson, Kevin Karlson, France and Liz Kehas-Dewaghe, Adam and Gina Kent, Tiffany Kersten, Derek and Jeannette Lovitch, Tim Lucas, Tom Magarian, Max Malmquist, Mike Malmquist, Becky Marvil, Kevin McLaughlin, Steve Mlodinow, Josh Nemeth, Evan Obercian, Michael O'Brien, Bryant Olsen, Bill Pranty, Michael Retter, Melissa Roach, Roy Rodriguez, Scott Schuette, Luke Seitz, Willie Sekula, Joel and Vicki Simons, David Simpson, James Smith, Ron Smith, Andrew Spencer, Brian Sullivan, David Swaim, Clay Taylor, Dave Tetlow, Bill Tweit, Scott Watson, Ron Weeks, Dustin Welch, Chris Wood, Andres Vasquez, and Chris Vogel.

My wife, Allison Anholt, not only helped by editing my work before it was fit for anyone else to see, but also by contributing greatly to the conservation section, index, and bibliography. Most importantly she helped guide me through some of the most difficult moments in my life and taught me that perfection is the enemy of done. This book is done because of you.

Ken Behrens, Steve Howell, Tony Leukering, and Derek Lovitch all improved the book with their knowledge and shaped the final form of this guide. I greatly appreciate your efforts, your time, and your thoughtful commentary.

The backbone of a photographic guide is clearly its photographs. A number of very talented photographers allowed their work to be included in this guide. Each and every one of them made an invaluable contribution to this guide and patiently put up with numerous emails from me throughout the process. I thank and appreciate all of you. Jesse Amesbury, George Armistead, Ken Behrens, Robin Corcoran, Hallie Daly, Mark Daly, Ian Davies, Jason Denesevich, Alix d'Entremont, Ted D'Eon, Thomas Ford-Hutchinson, Reinhard Geisler, Doug Gochfeld, John Groskopf, Luis Guillermo, Dan Irizarry, Jean Iron, Daniel Irons, Zbigniew Kajzer, Kevin Karlson, Mark Lockwood, Jeannette Lovitch, Roy Lowe, Paul Mason, Tammy McQuade, Trey Mitchell, Marky Mutchler, Michael Ostrowski, James Pawlicki, Lukasz Pulawski, Nick Ransdale, Daniel J. Riley, Patricia Rojo, Cameron Rutt, Cathy Sheeter, Andrew Spencer, Victor Stoll, Brian Sullivan, Jerry Ting, Scott Watson, Dustin Welch, and Hans Wohlmuth.

Finally the team at Princeton University Press and D & N Publishing all did incredible work shepherding this guide to the finish line. You are all greatly appreciated: Kyle Carlsen, Karen L. Carter, Robert Kirk, Penny Mansley, Megan Mendonca, Dr. David Price-Goodfellow, and everyone behind the scenes.



Published by Princeton University Press
41 William Street, Princeton, New Jersey 08540
99 Banbury Road, Oxford OX2 6JX

press.princeton.edu



ISBN (pbk.) 978-0-691-16187-7
ISBN (e-book) 978-0-691-25331-2

Library of Congress Control Number: 2023938879

British Library Cataloging-in-Publication Data is available

Editorial: Robert Kirk and Megan Mendonça
Production Editorial: Karen Carter
Text Design: D & N Publishing, Wiltshire, UK
Jacket/Cover Design: Wanda España
Production: Steven Sears
Publicity: Caitlyn Robson and Matthew Taylor
Copyeditor: Kyle Carlsen

Jacket/Cover Credit: Jacket photography by Cameron Cox

This book has been composed in Brandon Grotesque

Printed on acid-free paper. ∞

Printed in China

10 9 8 7 6 5 4 3 2 1

# CONTENTS

COMMON TERN June, NS. Alix d'Entremont. Terns are as dynamic as they are beautiful, and time spent observing them is always a pleasure.

# INTRODUCTION TO TERNS AND SKIMMERS

Terns are a stunning group of birds, unmatched in their elegant mastery of the air, possessing striking behaviors and performing incredible feats of migration. They are similar to their close cousins, gulls, in being easy to observe. However, they lack much of the angst, most of the hybridization, and all of the regular visits to garbage dumps associated with gulls; instead, they tend to prefer idyllic wave-bathed beaches. They just might be the most perfect group of birds!

As with gulls, though, the birding community tends to perceive terns as a difficult group to identify. This stigma holds even though most terns are quite distinctive and true identification challenges are few. Rather than bolster that reputation, and thereby justify the existence of this book, let's instead take a moment to debunk it. When you actually look at which species present true identification challenges, it quickly becomes clear that the reputation terns have for being a difficult group stems largely from just a few species. Even birders with very little experience with the group can quickly learn to recognize most terns.

While a few species do present legitimate identification quandaries, some study and a modest outlay of time observing birds in the field can rapidly lead to proficiency even with the difficult *Sterna* terns. The challenges with identifying terns are quite digestible, offering just enough difficulty to be stimulating without becoming frustrating, if approached correctly.

INTRO 1 Brown Noddy. April, FL. Noddies and skimmers have a number of behavioral and anatomic traits that differ distinctly from terns. Skimmers have been recognized as a subfamily distinct from terns, and it seems likely that, in the future, noddies will be considered taxonomically distinct from terns as well. Noddies and skimmers are included in this guide because they have traditionally been associated with terns and because their beauty enhances this guide.

This guide was written to provide that correct approach to the challenging species and to cut away the perception of difficulty where it is undeserved. The goal is to simplify, not to complicate. Most importantly, the aim is to build the confidence of the reader by providing field-proven methods for identifying terns.

This book is not targeted at the expert but is instead designed to usher the birder who has previously never fully mastered the identification of terns to a level of comfort and proficiency. While this guide is first and foremost an identification resource, it is also a celebration of a charismatic group of birds well worth celebrating.

## WHAT'S INCLUDED

This guide treats the terns, skimmers, and noddies of North America north of the Mexican border, covering nineteen species: sixteen species of terns, two species of noddies, and Black Skimmer. Sixteen of these species breed within the region (though Bridled Tern does so irregularly and in very small numbers), while one species, Black Noddy, is a regular stray in very low numbers to the Dry Tortugas, and two species, White-winged and Whiskered Terns, are true vagrants to North America from the Old World. Large-billed Tern is excluded from the guide. Although it has occurred in this region as frequently as Whiskered Tern (three times for both), its history of vagrancy is far less recent than that of Whiskered Tern and it is essentially an unmistakable species; the only thing that really needs to be said about Large-billed Tern is that if you happen to see a big tern with a huge yellow bill and a Sabine's Gull–like wing pattern in North America, you are having a really good day.

## TAXONOMY

Currently both the American Ornithological Society (AOS) and *The Clements Checklist of Birds of the World* include all species in this guide as part of the family Laridae within the order Charadriiformes. Charadriiformes includes shorebirds, alcids, and jaegers as distant relatives of our subject species. More closely related, the family Laridae includes three subfamilies: Larinae, or gulls; Sterninae, or terns and noddies; and Rynchopinae, or skimmers. This guide excludes gulls, for which many guides have been written, and instead focuses on the other subfamilies of Laridae. Skimmers were long considered part of terns but differ in numerous ways, and their recent recognition as a distinct subfamily acknowledges these differences. Issues of taxonomy are rarely neat though, and some recent genetic studies have indicated that within the family Laridae, noddies are at least as distinct as skimmers, perhaps more so, and the current taxonomic arrangement of subfamilies within Laridae is very likely to change in the future to reflect this. Regarding the recognition of species and subspecies, this guide follows the *Clements Checklist* as of April 2022, though I will occasionally mention the opinions of other taxonomic authorities where deemed interesting.

## IDENTIFICATION

*Size.* Identification starts with size. There is a frequent misconception that size is difficult to judge in the field, and size as an identification trait is often downplayed in bird identification literature. This approach is wrong. Particularly on a macro level, most humans are quite good at judging relative size within the context of their environment. We've done it hundreds of times a day for our entire lives, and the better we know the setting in which we are making judgments, the better our relative judgments of size become. This is, essentially, an innate, subconscious skill. The confusion comes from the fact that we tend to be poor at transferring judgments of relative size into a standardized system of measurements such as inches or feet unless we have received specific training on how to do so. For example, a Least Tern will immediately strike most observers as a small tern, but asking ten people to guess the exact size of the bird they are observing will likely result in quite a broad range of guesses, most incorrect. Such an error will likely lead to the belief that the observers judge size poorly. Accurately placing an object into an arbitrary human scale, though, is not the skill that matters when it comes to judging the size of a bird. What we need to be able to do well is to make size judgments in relation to other objects in the surrounding environment. This is a skill you are likely far better at than you give yourself credit for.

That is not to say that size judgments are infallible. Sometimes circumstances converge to cause us to make a relative size judgment that is far off the mark, leading to a misidentification. Often such size misjudgments and the resulting errors are glaring and potentially embarrassing so we tend to remember them clearly. This human tendency to remember failures more clearly than successes, and to remember major failures most clearly of all, feeds the narrative that size is an unreliable trait. This causes us to ignore the thousands of times our instinctive ability to judge relative size has subtly guided us to the correct identification, as these instances do not stand out as clearly as the few times a misjudgment of size epically misled us. The successes that result from using relative size as a cornerstone trait when identifying birds far exceed the mistakes it occasionally produces.

Instinctively judging size as described above is essentially judging it on a macro level. It is a rapid, almost unconscious process, though with practice in different light conditions and at different distances you can refine and improve this natural process. It is essentially assessing perceived length, height, and mass all at once and coming up with an instinctive, cumulative judgment for these metrics. Judging size on a micro level, such as estimating the difference in size

INTRO 2 Common Terns (in the early stages of prebasic molt) with Bonaparte's Gulls. Sept., OH. Flocks of Common Terns in the fall show a bewildering array of plumages. However, the size and structure are the same for all, so by identifying one bird and then comparing it to the rest of the terns in the flock, you essentially identify all the terns in this flock regardless of plumage.

INTRO 3 Least Terns, Black Tern, and a Royal Tern. Aug., FL. Most terns are extremely gregarious, a fortunate tendency for birders as it allows us to gauge size and structure in the easiest way possible: by direct comparison. The Royal Tern, the second largest tern in the region, towers over the Least and Black Terns, the two smallest. Note that while the Black Tern is only very slightly longer-bodied than the Least Terns surrounding it, it appears clearly larger as it stands taller, and the impression is reinforced by its dark color.

between Forster's and Common Terns, involves first recognizing that the size difference, though subtle, can often be perceived and applied in the field—knowledge won through careful, repeated observation. Once this fact is acknowledged, you can start recognizing the limits of individual variation and where sizes may overlap between species, identifying when the difference can only be attributed to birds belonging to distinct species and, conversely, when this identification trait will be unreliable. Accurate size judgments on this micro level are a conscious, learned process, as opposed to the instinctive process utilized by macro-level judgments. When an observer is dealing with particularly small differences, such as those between Forster's and Common Terns, size judgments are most easily applied when directly comparing similar species. Thinking about size on a micro level can be very useful even when observing a group of birds that are all the same size, as experience will tell you that Forster's Terns differ enough in size from Common Terns that a flock with both will not appear uniform in size. A flock in which all members are the same size can only be either all Forster's Terns or all Common Terns. For species that the observer knows particularly well, even the size of a lone bird can be judged, though with less certainty than with direct comparisons. Unlike macro size judgments, which can be useful at most distances, these more refined size assessments are most effective at close to moderate distances. These macro and micro size judgments, though they operate very differently, prove to be beneficial in conjunction with each other. Macro judgments are useful in cutting a huge list of possible species down to a manageable number. Micro judgments can then be utilized to refine the list further, and are particularly useful within groups of similar birds, such as when identifying *Sterna* terns.

One situation where your size judgments can mislead you, though, is when you are primed to look for a specific size difference and there is a significant value ascribed to perceiving that size difference. For example, let's say you were looking for your lifer Arctic Tern amid Common Terns, and one of the traits you are looking for is the smaller size of Arctic. In such a situation, you very likely will be prone to noticing differences in size that you might have easily overlooked if the idea of an Arctic Tern in the area hadn't primed your mind, creating a hyperawareness of minor differences in size. It is wise to be wary of your ability to judge all traits objectively, including size, as desire can distort how we perceive our world.

*Structure*. The second layer in the identification process is assessing structure. Size and structure become more useful when considered in conjunction with each other, and many birds can be identified this way without the use of any other traits. For example, Caspian Tern can be instantly identified in most situations by size and structure alone. As with size, structure works best when considered in two parts: the rapid overview of structure that allows you to instantaneously do some basic categorization, such as separating a tern from a gull, and the careful, deliberate evaluations of structure needed to discern the differences between a Common and an Arctic Tern. I'll use the terms "macro" and "micro" structure to delineate which type of structure is being discussed.

The macro level would generally consider things like the long, angular, pointed wings; lean bodies; and sharply pointed bills that, even at a distance, allow for rapid classification. On the macro level of structure, we can, with little more than a

INTRO 4 Caspian, Common, and Sandwich Terns with Black Skimmers and Laughing Gulls. Sept., GA. Terns often gather in mixed flocks with other species of terns and other waterbirds. These situations are ideal for learning size differences and comparing the structures of different species.

glance, take a distant flying object and place it into a much more defined category, greatly simplifying the identification process. For observers with intermediate or better experience, this classification is largely subconscious and instantaneous, a product of recognition. For beginners, it may take some thought initially, but with even a modest amount of practice, recognition of familiar groups of birds will begin to take hold. On flying birds, all else being equal, smaller birds generally have faster wingbeats. The difference in the speed of the wingbeats between Least and Caspian Terns is an extreme example, while the difference between the wingbeats of Sooty and Bridled Terns is a key identification trait. In general, the speed of wingbeats contributes greatly to size perception, and often makes it easier to judge the size of a distant flying bird than that of a motionless bird.

Once we have evaluated structure on the macro level and determined we are looking at a tern, the real fun begins. Just as micro size assessments require careful observation, judging structure on a micro level requires critical examination and knowledge, becoming more effective with increased experience. It requires exact knowledge of the expected traits of each species it is being applied to and the range of structural variability each species can display. Unless, of course, you are blessed with the opportunity to directly compare species. Then all you need to do is look. Such opportunities should be treated like gold mines and visually harvested to the greatest extent possible as they are, bar none, the best opportunities for long-term learning. Over time, your ability to judge micro structure will increase, and structural traits that were once subtle and easily overlooked will become obvious, or even nearly second nature. This more nuanced perception of structure is one of the major steps in transforming bird identification from a difficult slog into something more akin to an art form.

*Using flocks*. Size and structure are essential traits in bird identification, and the best way to assess and learn both is to view mixed flocks of similar species. Fortunately, terns are gregarious and frequently occur in flocks of multiple species alongside gulls and other waterbirds, creating ideal comparisons. Birders are often taught to treat every bird as a standalone identification, to use field marks to figure out the bird in question, and then to start the process over with the next bird. This process is tedious and repetitive; instead, start by finding the species you immediately recognize. Using a known bird as a starting point allows you to much more accurately assess traits of any unknown species or individuals by leveraging comparisons. The size, structure, and plumage traits of an unknown species will have a more meaningful context when compared to those of a bird whose identity you know, rather than assessed independently. Once you have nailed down the identity of an unknown bird, look around carefully for others with the same size and structure. You can infer that they are the same species and potentially thereby identify multiple individuals while only going through the detailed process of puzzling out the initial bird. This is particularly useful with flocks of migrant terns as they often show a myriad of plumage variations.

*Process of elimination*. Process of elimination is not typically emphasized in bird identification but can be very valuable when actively employed. This is particularly true in flocks of terns as, after judging size on a macro level you will, at most, have four similar species to separate. By using process of

INTRO 5 Royal Tern. April, TX. The contrast between the fresh six inner primaries and four older outer primaries is called a "molt limit." As the white powdery "bloom" wears off the older outer four primaries, a visible dark wedge develops. P7 is the oldest feather and is clearly the darkest, while P10 (the outermost primary) is the freshest of the outer four and clearly paler than the other three as it has lost less of its bloom. Notice how the pale tongues (retained bloom) on P8 and P9 have the exact shapes of the primaries that rest on top of them. When birds fold their wings, each primary protects most of the primary underneath it. In terns, this protection is often made visible by a pattern of retained bloom.

elimination, the choices can be whittled down to one or two quite rapidly.

## MOLT, AGING, AND FEATHER WEAR

Molt is, at its most basic level, feather growth. Because feathers are essential to birds for flight and temperature regulation, molt is a significant aspect of a bird's life. Molt occurs in predictable waves in most species on something that roughly corresponds to an annual cycle, the new feather growth (molt) pushing out old feathers, thus regularly refreshing a bird's plumage. Molt can cause significant changes in how a bird appears, and therefore is of interest to those who study birds. While feather growth is a simple concept to understand, how molt has evolved in different groups of birds and different species is varied and complex. It remains a subject about which much is still to be learned, which is exciting, yet can also be intimidating to many birders. The focus of this guide is tern identification, and to best identify terns, it is helpful to know at least a few basics about tern molt, as terns are one of the groups of birds that have evolved some unique traits in their molt that influence identification.

*Basics: Color change and patterns in tern primaries.* To fully understand all the nuances of tern appearance, an excellent grasp of tern molt is a must. Most terns, though, can be identified without a deep knowledge of molt. Indeed, specific knowledge of tern molt is likely to be the difference between a misidentification and a correct identification in far less than 1% of the terns encountered. There is, though, some basic knowledge that can greatly aid your ability to process the range of variability you will encounter while observing terns:

1. Terns that are largely pale (most terns) have black primaries covered in pale "powder" (see below for complete description) that makes them appear white or silvery.
2. No matter the time of year a primary is acquired, this pale powder is densest when the primary is freshly molted, and it then wears off slowly, thus gradually exposing the black base color underneath. As wear occurs the primary will first appear pale gray, then dark gray, then fully black as the powder wears off completely. How quickly the powder wears off depends on how much was on the feather to begin with, and this varies by species and by individual. This wear is not evenly distributed—areas on a feather that are more exposed to the elements will darken faster than areas on the feather that are shielded by overlapping feathers. Primaries transitioning from pale to dark due to wear is a unique trait and the opposite of what is seen in gulls.
3. Many terns, most notably Common Tern, molt some inner primaries in the late winter/spring. This means that in summer the new inner primaries will still be very pale, while the powder is almost worn off the older outer primaries, making them appear much darker than the pale inner primaries. A new primary side by side with an old primary creates an obvious light–dark contrast, called a "molt contrast" or "molt limit," that becomes more and more apparent as the powder wears off the older primary, exposing the black base color. Eventually, the older outer primaries will appear entirely black. At this point, the outer primaries cannot continue to darken, but the inner primaries can, and they will eventually also become black, "catching up" to the outer primaries and making the molt limit difficult to see. Often a new wave of molt sweeps through the primaries, renewing them before the inner primaries fully catch up to the outer primaries, but in some species, like Common Tern, some

individuals will show entirely dark primaries in the fall before new molted feathers, covered in fresh pale powder, restart the process.

4. The amount of powder on the primaries and the number of inner primaries molted in spring vary by species of tern, causing discernable, species-specific tendencies as to what time of year and where in the primaries the molt limit will be visible. These tendencies are often strong enough to be widely recognized field identification traits, such as the dark wedge in the wings of Common Tern.
5. While these traits are useful, there is also tremendous individual variability to consider. Common Tern, for example, typically molts five inner primaries in spring, so the molt limit appears right in the middle of the primaries and is typically visible from early summer through fall. Some Common Terns, though, molt 7–8 inner primaries in the spring, which means the molt limit will appear farther out on the wing as it becomes visible later in the year. Some terns have more or less powder on the primaries, thus slowing down or speeding up the time line on when molt limits become visible. Some Common Terns show an obvious molt limit as early as April, while others (those with feathers covered with a greater amount of white powder) show almost no perceivable molt limit in the primaries through the entire summer. As with all tern identification traits, tendencies driven by molt can be useful and reliable while still falling short of being absolute. Expect and appreciate the variation.

*Molt details.* Flight feather molt in terns is among the most complex in any group of birds. This complexity is often uniquely displayed in terns because in most species the primaries darken noticeably as they wear. As most birds molt primaries one by one in a sequential order, from the innermost (P1) to the outermost (P10 in terns), the freshest, palest primaries are always alongside the darkest, oldest primaries. This location where two generations of feathers are side by side is a "molt limit" or "molt contrast" (referenced above). In most species of birds molt limits are quite subtle, often visible only in the hand, but the molt limits in the primaries of terns are often obvious. This allows birders to identify patterns in the molts of terns and to watch their progression far more easily than with sandpipers, for example.

Discussion of molt necessitates discussion of wear, as feather wear is what makes molt necessary. Sunlight and windblown sand and dirt particles are the primary agents of wear, and will eventually, without a fresh wave of molt, wear feathers away entirely. Wear is particularly apparent on large, easily observed flight feathers. The flight feathers of terns have an interesting adaptation that mitigates the normal effects of wear on feathers. The main central support of a feather is called the "feather shaft." The hundreds of stiff little branches that stick out on either side of the shaft and make up most of the surface area of the feather are called "barbs." The barbs are covered in tiny barbules. In most species of terns, the barbules on the flight feathers are covered in frilled growths so fine it almost appears that the feathers are covered in a fine powder. This powder, sometimes referred to as "bloom," is the powder referenced above in points 1–5. Thus, the bloom protects the integrity of the primaries, shielding them from wear until the bloom is worn away. The difference can be seen when comparing terns to other large waterbirds with black outer primaries. In species such as gulls,

**INTRO 6** Typical Northern Hemisphere primary patterns in Common Tern. The images show the most typical primary appearance at different times of the year. Some individuals will be out of step with this norm, however, showing a pattern more typical of a different time of year.
***Spring:*** *Primaries appear uniformly pale (April), though molt limit in the middle primaries is typically visible if seen well. Some individuals may show a low-contrast, darker outer primary wedge throughout the spring, but by the end of spring, most Common Terns show a visible but low-contrast dark wedge (May).*
***Summer:*** *By midsummer, most individuals show an easily visible dark outer primary wedge (July), though some may still show the late spring pattern (May) or, rarely, show very little wedge (April).*
***Fall:*** *Like summer, but the dark outer primary wedge is often entirely black. Perched birds appear to have entirely blackish primaries, as the paler inner primaries are hidden in this posture (Sept.). Some will show a more muted outer primary wedge, while small numbers show a very subtle wedge (May).*

which lack bloom, a freshly molted black primary is subject to wear and fading as soon as it is acquired, often fading to brown or even tan before it is replaced by the next wave of molt. In terns, typically, once the bloom is worn off, the next wave of molt occurs shortly thereafter, and the primaries are replaced before the black base feather can fade or wear significantly. The exception is the noddies, which show patterns of wear very similar to those of gulls: their outer primaries wear to paler brown and the wing coverts of immature birds often show extreme wear.

INTRO 7 Forster's Tern. Sept., NJ. This Forster's Tern is actively molting its flight feathers as part of its complete prebasic molt. While Common Terns and some Roseate and Arctic Terns may molt a few inner primaries in fall, these species are unlikely to be found in North America at this advanced stage of wing molt. Due to the duration of Arctic Tern's migration, Forster's Terns have completed their primary molt before Arctic Terns have begun their primary molt.

## MOLTS AND PLUMAGES TERMINOLOGY

In order to understand molts and plumages, you must have a framework for comparing molts, and a naming system that allows molts to be identified provides the framework. Ornithologists have used a variety of different terminology systems to describe molt over the years. These systems tended to be heavily influenced by the regions in which they were developed, making them difficult to apply outside those regions (e.g., using terms based on Northern Hemisphere seasonality to describe the plumages of a bird that spends more than half of its year in the Southern Hemisphere). The Humphrey and Parkes system (H&P system) (Humphrey and Parkes 1959) addressed this issue by creating terms that could be applied universally with no connection to seasonality or breeding status. The Humphrey and Parkes system was later updated by Howell et al. (2003), creating the modified Humphrey and Parkes terminology, the best framework currently in existence for studying the specifics of molts and plumages.

One concept that originated with the H&P system and was further popularized by Howell et al. is the concept of the molt cycle, or just "cycle." A molt cycle is begun when a molt begins and it continues until that same molt occurs again, signaling the end of one cycle and the beginning of the next. Since, in most species, molts occur on roughly a yearly basis, a molt cycle is typically about a year long. It is now widely accepted and understood to describe a gull as, for example, a first-cycle Western Gull, and while this method is most frequently applied to gulls, it is just as useful for describing terns. Using the terminology of cycles to describe immature birds is particularly useful, as immature birds are far more likely than adult birds to have molt cycles that are shorter or longer than a year. As soon as a new molt begins, the next cycle begins, thus avoiding awkward situations like describing a nine-month-old bird as a "second-year Royal Tern."

While the Humphrey and Parkes system is an effective one for studying molts, most casual birders are not studying molts, and the inconsistences that arise when attempting to universally apply terms tethered to seasonality and breeding status are of little concern. The inertia and convenience of long-used terms like "breeding" and "nonbreeding" and "summer plumage" and "winter plumage" have kept those terms in use, and they are in fact more used within the birding world than are those of the Humphrey and Parkes system.

Because the H&P terminology is not widely understood by most birders and the inertia of familiarity continues to propel more traditional plumage and aging terminology, in this guide, traditional plumage and aging terms are used with H&P in parentheses. The terms used are as follows:

### *ADULTS*

*Nonbreeding.* Fairly self-explanatory. This is the appearance North American terns have during the Northern Hemisphere's winter, when many of these terns are not in North America. Most North American terns have more white on their heads and in many species whiter bodies. It is most comparable to "basic plumage" in the H&P system.

*Basic.* "Adult (definitive) basic" is an H&P system term most comparable to "nonbreeding adult." It is used in the guide in parentheses. Basic plumage is brought about by a prebasic molt, which is a complete or near-complete molt in which all feathers are replaced. As the name suggests, basic plumage is the most standard plumage. It is shared by all species of birds. If a species molts only once a year, it goes from one basic plumage to the next. As terns are fairly large and dependent on their ability to fly to obtain food, it is inevitable that they would need to undergo slow, protracted molts that take months to complete. How they fit such periods into their yearly schedule varies dramatically by species. The *Thalasseus* terns and Least Tern get an early start, with their prebasic molt beginning as early as June and overlapping with the breeding season, pausing (also known as "molt suspension") for migration, and then finishing in the fall. Arctic Tern, on the other hand, doesn't begin the prebasic molt until December, after arriving at its nonbreeding haunts along the ice shelves of the Antarctic, taking advantage of rich food sources there to fuel a more rapid molt that may be completed very quickly.

*Breeding.* This is the appearance North American terns have during the Northern Hemisphere's summer. Most North American terns have black caps, and some acquire gray or black bodies and long tail-streamers. "Breeding plumage" is most comparable to "alternate plumage" in the H&P system.

*Alternate.* "Adult (definitive) alternate" is an H&P system term most comparable to "adult breeding." It is used in the guide in parentheses and abbreviated to "alt." Alternate plumage is brought about by a prealternate molt. While many species of birds lack an alternate plumage, all North American terns except noddies have an alternate plumage. In most species with an alternate plumage the prealternate molt does not include flight feathers. Terns, however, are overachievers, and many species replace large chunks of their flight feathers in the prealternate molt—up to nine primaries in Least Tern! In traditional terminology, this is most comparable to "breeding plumage."

### *IMMATURES*

*Juvenile plumage.* "Juvenile plumage" is a term used both in the traditional terminologies and in the H&P system. It refers to the first coat of true feathers a bird acquires after its downy plumage. Juvenile plumage was redefined as "first-basic plumage" by Howell et al. (2003), as it is the first complete molt a bird undergoes. From a life-cycle-of-the-bird perspective, redefining juvenile plumage in this way allows it to fall in line with all subsequent basic plumages. From an identification-in-the-field perspective, juvenile plumage is distinct enough to warrant special attention. In terns, juvenile feathers on the crown, back, wing coverts, and tertials are often marked with a buffy reddish or brownish wash, while some of these feathers may have dark centers or dark subterminal markings that are unique to juvenile plumage. All of these markings are subject to incredibly rapid alterations by wear and fading, so a freshly fledged tern will often be dramatically more heavily marked than it will be a week or two later, and after another month it may look like a different bird entirely. This all happens through the action of sun and sand alone, and not due to molt. In juvenile terns, subtle washes of color, such as a buff wash in the crown, are altered most rapidly, quickly fading to pure white. Subterminal dark markings on the mantle feathers and tertials fade until they can be almost imperceptible by fall, while black feather centers fade to gray, but tend not to disappear entirely. This rapid change is difficult to fully illustrate in a guide. The figure below shows several stages of the alteration of the appearance of juvenile Least Terns, which is a good representation of the changes most juvenile pale terns undergo.

*First-cycle/second-cycle.* Categorizing birds by cycle rather than by specific plumage is an acknowledgment that it is often difficult to age birds in the field accurately and precisely.

**INTRO 8** Juvenile Least Terns. Early July, late July, and Aug., FL. These images show the transition from a very recently fledged juvenile (left) with a buffy wash to the crown, back, and wing coverts, to a juvenile that is several weeks older (center) that has already lost the buffy wash, to an early fall bird with the wing panel worn almost white and having already replaced a few back feathers (right). This demonstrates the lightning quick transition juvenile terns undergo due to the wear and fading of the brown/buffy wash most display at fledging. As the first plumage cycle progresses, their appearance will continue to evolve due to a complex series of molts as well as additional feather wear.

INTRO 9 Breeding adult Roseate and Common Terns. July, ME. Direct comparison, again, is a great aid in evaluating these two similar species. They are essentially the same size, but our brains will not perceive them so, and will see the Roseate Tern as smaller, as it is more lightly built. Also compare bill structure, which is similar but perceptively different: slightly thinner and more sharply pointed in the Roseate. If possible, though, take the easy route! One of these birds is glowing like it swallowed a light bulb. Roseate Tern shows this incandescent quality to a far greater extent than any other small or medium-sized tern, and even at a distance, this glowing quality is easily observable.

Sometimes it is better to use a term like "first-cycle" that is less precise but also less prone to error. "First-cycle" refers to the period from juvenile plumage until the beginning of the second basic molt. "Second-cycle" refers to the period from the second basic molt until the third basic molt, when most terns acquire adult or adult-like plumage. Calling a tern a "first-cycle Royal Tern" is similar to calling it a "first-year Royal Tern"; however, the use of cycles is tailored more to the individual bird, since it becomes a "second-cycle Royal Tern" as soon as it begins the second prebasic molt, be that in May or July. This is opposed to using the month of June to arbitrarily transition from first-year to second-year, as is often done in the life year system, in which a "first-year Royal Tern" in late May would become a "second-year Royal Tern" in June regardless of whether there has been any change in its appearance or molt.

*First-summer/second-summer type.* It is strongly preferable to not use terms connected to Northern Hemisphere seasons, particularly for terns, as many species occur in both hemispheres. However, much of the early literature on tern identification used this terminology, and so the idea of what a "first-summer Arctic Tern" is supposed to look like is well established. For this reason, these terms are used in the guide, although altered slightly: instead of "first-summer Arctic Tern," the term "first-summer type Arctic Tern" is used. We have learned that a bird that has the appearance of a "classic first-summer" Arctic Tern may be a year old, or it may be two years old or even three years old. Appearance is tied much less to physical age than is currently acknowledged, and our ability to determine actual age in the field is zero. By using "first-summer type Arctic Tern," we can still harness the mental picture evoked by the words "first-summer" while acknowledging that significant uncertainty exists as to the bird's true age.

## PLUMAGE-BASED IDENTIFICATION

Identification using plumage traits is well understood. How birders use plumage to make correct bird identifications is well understood and does not need further discussion. How birders become too dependent on plumage and how this all too often results in misidentifications, however, is worth a quick overview. In many cases, birders who struggle with terns do so because their approach to terns has been to learn one or two plumage traits per species and then to rely too heavily on this limited arsenal. While tern identification is not particularly difficult, it can seem immensely difficult if you take such an approach, since just about every plumage trait varies seasonally and individually. Terns, particularly the more difficult ones, are a group with precious few one-punch-knockout field marks. Instead, you should aim to develop your ability to blend multiple traits—plumage, structure, size, and the typical patterns produced by molt and wear—and to correctly assess which traits to weight more heavily for a particular situation or individual tern. You don't key these birds out or check off a couple of field marks and expect success. The process of tern identification is more akin to an art form than a cut-and-dry procedure.

That said, for difficult groups of birds, plumage traits are indeed the final piece of the puzzle to reach solid identifications. Focus particularly on the distribution of black on the head, as this can be helpful for most species year-round. For pale species, you also want to observe the amount and pattern of black on the wings. For breeding adults, the distribution and intensity of the gray on the underparts can be useful, but be aware that shades of gray are particularly affected by light conditions.

## VOCALIZATIONS

The value of learning the vocalizations of birds that reside in forests or other dense environments with low visibility is well understood. In contrast, learning the vocalizations of birds that are often in the open and can be easily viewed is often neglected, yet being able to identify and quickly hone in on a scarce or rare species is as valuable on a beach as it is in a forest. The value becomes apparent when the harsh, disyllabic call of a Roseate Tern cuts through the din of Common Terns, allowing you to see and appreciate a beautiful species that you might have otherwise missed.

Fortunately, the basic vocalizations of most terns are easy to learn. The throaty *Ke-YOWs* of adult Caspian Terns and the harsh, rolling calls of Royal Terns are unmistakable. Knowing *Sterna* vocalizations makes the plumage-based identification challenges of that group irrelevant, bestowing a huge advantage in picking out rare species. Juvenile *Thalasseus* terns and Caspian Terns have loud begging vocalizations that they give for months after fledging, allowing the observer to both identify and age them instantly. During your next encounter with terns, spend a little time focusing on their vocalizations—it will be time well spent.

## LIGHTING

The quality and angle of light factor into every identification we make. It is a complicating component that can easily cause

INTRO 10 Common Tern. April, TX. Notice how just the shadow of the wing enhances the darkness of the gray chest. The effect can be even stronger under darker conditions. The subtle grays that make up the plumage of most terns are particularly prone to appear altered by lighting. Shadow dramatically enhances grays, while strong sunlight washes it out equally dramatically. Terns are often found in open habitats where shadow, strong sunlight, and reflected light from pale sand or water is commonplace. Spending time watching terns allows observers to appreciate these challenges.

**INTRO 11** Common Tern. July, ME. Hallie Daly. Lighting affects every bird identification we make. Light as poor as this could potentially allow us to shut off the part of the brain that is constantly bombarding us with information about color, and instead carefully evaluate the structure of this Common Tern, thereby learning something about the bird we didn't know before. Or, it could be the trigger we need to take a moment to enjoy the beauty of birds and the joy of being outside.

observers to misjudge what they are seeing. Fortunately, our brains automatically adjust for lighting conditions as they process what our eyes see, rather than overreacting to dark or pale colors created by strong shadows or sun bleaching. We may still misjudge a bird's appearance due to tricks of the light, but the more that we recognize these errors, the more that we tend to improve in our ability to compensate for lighting conditions. Terns are a bit of a special case, though. They are often found in habitats with strong sunlight, like beaches and open marshes, where the addition of reflection off sand or water can be a compounding factor. Their plumage is largely subtle shades of gray, a color that is easily bleached out in strong sunlight. There is really nothing you can do about this other than to be aware that it is an issue. Practice looking at terns in strong light to see the effects firsthand, and then compensate for them, and realize that, under some conditions, you will have to reduce the distance at which you make identifications in order to reduce error.

Be aware that a pale bird appears larger against a dark background, and smaller against a pale background, while the reverse to true for a dark bird. Similarly, backlit birds seem smaller, and birds in low light often appear larger, though low light will also make the wingbeats appear faster, which can affect how you judge size.

Finally, lighting is a major factor when attempting to identify terns in photos. Our finely honed ability to subconsciously compensate for lighting conditions in the field is worthless when viewing photos, and this is one of the major reasons why birds in photos can be more difficult to identify than birds in the field. Again, there is very little you can do about this other than to take things more slowly when trying to identify a difficult bird from a photo. The bird's not going anywhere; take the time to triple-check all traits. Also, while you cannot subconsciously judge the light, look at the orientation of shadows and other lighting clues to attempt to consciously judge lighting.

## PROBABILITY

Probability is essentially the insider trading of bird identification, except no one goes to jail. Understanding what species to expect at a particular location in each season puts an observer in a very advantageous position for identification even before looking at a single bird. For highly migratory species, like terns, that often have very precise patterns of seasonal occurrence, this is particularly true. Process of elimination is weighted toward the species that are most expected. The more precisely you can learn patterns of distribution and seasonal occurrence, the more effective your "insider trades" will be.

Although you can start learning distribution from a book like this or from the range maps of a field guide, the more regional your sources of information are, the more precise they are likely to be. Check to see what resources your state or local birding organization have available; ideally, you are looking for a bar chart of seasonal occurrence that can lay out the species expected week by week. For areas that receive frequent coverage by birders, eBird.org can be a fantastic source of information on distribution and seasonal occurrence patterns. Everyone admires Martha Stewart—be like Martha and use all the insider trading information available to you.

## HYBRIDS

In stark contrast to gulls, hybridization in terns is far less common, though still more frequent than in many other families of birds. Unfortunately, it happens infrequently enough that it receives no coverage in standard field guides. In many cases, the impetus for hybridization in terns seems to be vagrant individuals with no same-species choice in mate. North American tern hybrids are almost exclusively intrageneric hybrids, with the genera of *Sterna*, *Chlidonias*, and *Thalasseus* being the ones open to adventure. The only known intergeneric hybrid is from a single report of a Forster's x Gull-billed Tern hybrid.

The crested terns, *Thalasseus*, hybridize rarely but regularly, and are a good example of hybridization brought on by vagrancy. The most famous example is the occurrence of multiple Elegant Terns in western Europe and their subsequent hybridization with Eurasian Sandwich Terns. Concerns about the identification of such an unlikely vagrant to Europe caused three such birds to be captured, and DNA evidence definitively proved them to be Elegant Terns (Dufour et al. 2016). A similar situation occurred in Florida, where a vagrant Elegant Tern appeared in a colony of Sandwich Terns and produced hybrid offspring.

The Sea of Cortez/southern California presents an additional example of hybridization triggered by vagrancy in *Thalasseus* terns. In southern California, birds that seem consistent with Sandwich x Elegant Tern hybrids are rare but somewhat expected. Though there is one known mixed Elegant x Sandwich Tern pair from southern California, the majority of such birds likely come from Isla Rasa, the primary Elegant Tern nesting island in the Sea of Cortez. Researchers on Isla Rasa have documented dozens of birds showing traits consistent with Elegant x Sandwich Tern hybrids despite very few confirmed records of Sandwich Terns at this site (Velarde and Rojo 2012). Interestingly, birds with mixed characteristics appear to nest assortatively on Isla Rasa, which is extraordinarily improbable on an island that is essentially wall-to-wall Elegant Terns. Assortative pairing has, however, been documented in other hybrid terns, such as in Roseate x Common Tern hybrids in New York (Hays 1975).

INTRO 12 Common x Roseate Tern hybrid. June, NB. Ted D'Eon. This bird, banded as a chick, is a known hybrid. Tern hybridization is a subject that has received little attention from birders, as it is a relatively rare occurrence. Particularly among the very similar *Sterna* terns, it is likely that there are more hybrid individuals than we realize, and birders are just not equipped to key in on them.

In the Caribbean, the issue is not hybridization between species but intergradation, interbreeding between two subspecies. Cayenne Tern is a distinctive South American tern currently considered a subspecies of Sandwich Tern, but there is a broad intergrade zone in the southern Caribbean, with evidence that the intergrade zone is moving northward (Hayes 2004). Cayenne Tern is found quite rarely in the U.S., while birds with traits that are similar to Cayenne intergrades are much more regular, though still rare, in the Southeast. There are questions about whether some Sandwich Terns can show characteristics similar to Cayenne x Sandwich intergrades. Recent DNA analysis has suggested that Cayenne Tern is extremely similar to the North American Sandwich Tern, and so widespread intergradation is somewhat expected. For more information on *Thalasseus* tern hybridization, see page 55.

Unfortunately, hybridization among the already quite similar *Sterna* terns is among the most regular, particularly Common x Roseate, though all possible North American *Sterna* combinations have been recorded except for Roseate x Forster's. Still, such hybrids are quite rare. Ideally, potential *Sterna* hybrids should be photographed extensively, and an attempt should be made to record any vocalizations.

White-winged Tern provides an additional example of vagrancy driving hybridization. White-winged Terns have bred with Black Terns in Quebec and New York State, though neither nest fledged young.

Tern hybrids are a clear exception to the general rule that tern identification is mostly straightforward. The first difficulty is recognizing that you are dealing with a hybrid. Once that is established, the more difficult task of identifying *which* hybrid begins. Often the identification starts with noticing a bird that is an odd size or has aberrant structural features, then noting mismatched plumage traits. For example, *Thalasseus* hybrids often have oddly patterned bills. It is best to attempt to extensively photograph any suspected tern hybrid, including the spread wing, and to attempt to note vocalizations before beginning the evaluation process.

## LIFE HISTORY

The life histories of terns are interesting, varied, and largely beyond the scope of this guide. There are plenty of other resources available for those interested in tern ecology. Two of the best are Cornell's *Birds of the World Online* (www.birdsoftheworld.org) and *Terns* by Cabot and Nisbet (2013), a comprehensive book covering the ecology of the terns of the British Isles, all of which are also found in North America.

**INTRO 13** Arctic Tern. June, Iceland. Ken Behrens. The migration of Arctic Tern, an annual tour of the earth's oceans and polar regions covering roughly 25,000 miles, is the longest of any bird, and is one of the most spectacular feats in nature. From nesting amid lupines in the Arctic to foraging along the ice shelves of the Antarctic, Arctic Terns bask in more sunlight than any creature on earth.

## MIGRATION

Terns are shaped by flight, their bodies chiseled by life on the wind. Unsurprisingly, the family includes some of the world's most heralded migrants, headlined, of course, by the champion of bird migration, the Arctic Tern, whose meandering, pole-to-pole migration can cover 25,000 miles in a year. Common Terns are no slouches in their migratory distances either, and are known for performing "leap-frog migrations," meaning those that nest the farthest north also winter the farthest south, thus "leaping over" other Common Terns that nest in more southerly latitudes and also winter farther north. The Common Terns nesting in Scandinavia winter around the horn of Africa and take a circuitous route so that they nearly match many Arctic Terns in distance traveled. Not all migratory movements among terns are as classically north–south as those of Arctic and Common Terns. Some species, particularly the crested terns, disperse northward—often far north of their breeding range—after the breeding season. The first wave of this post-breeding dispersal is largely made up of failed breeders and immature birds, but these are soon augmented by breeders with loudly begging juveniles in tow. Elegant Terns can disperse as far north from their Gulf of California breeding range as the Pacific Northwest before turning around and migrating south as far as coastal Chile, another impressive feat of migration. Tropical terns, particularly Sooty Tern, often spend years wandering tropical oceans, rarely landing, and sleeping while on the wing.

Staging is a key aspect of migration for some terns. Many species gather in huge groups in the same locations year after year. In some species, terns gather in greater and greater numbers before leaving staging areas almost simultaneously. Roseate Terns in Cape Cod are a particularly good example of this; over approximately a week in mid-August, the numbers around Cape Cod go from thousands to practically zero. In contrast, Common Terns also stage in Cape Cod, but depart the staging areas more gradually, peaking in early to mid-September, but hundreds still remain into late October, with stragglers into December.

Unlike species of waterfowl, which often migrate in large flocks using distinct formations that signify migratory behavior, or species of raptors that gather in large kettles as they migrate, for most species of terns active migration can be difficult to discern. A Common Tern flying by could be fixed on a location hundreds or even thousands of miles away, or could just be commuting to the next bay. If, however, you observe a steady stream of terns all heading in the direction expected for that season's migration, in singles and small groups that often track along nearly the same flight path as prior individuals, that is active tern migration. An additional obstacle to observing tern migration is that some species—like Arctic and Roseate Terns and many Common and Black Terns—migrate well offshore, or migrate nocturnally at high altitude.

## CONSERVATION

While the primary purpose of this book is identification, taking a moment to appreciate the issues that face this beautiful group of birds is still essential. There are a variety of conservation challenges that face terns. In the 1800s and early 1900s, terns suffered almost to the point of local extinction from egg collection, hunting for the millinery (feather) trade, and subsistence harvesting of eggs and adults. While modern conservation legislature such as the Endangered Species Act and the Migratory Bird Treaty Act reduced these challenges, terns now need to overcome a variety of obstacles throughout their lives. Modern challenges range from the obvious, such as the development of coastal beaches and the draining or alteration of marshes, to the more insidious, such as climate change resulting in rising water levels, warming ocean temperatures changing the prey base, and introduced species, such as Zebra Mussels, altering habitat. On their breeding grounds, terns also often face issues of human disturbance, increased levels of predation by human-subsidized or introduced predators, and encroachment of gulls into favored nesting locations.

Due to their charisma, proximity to human habitation during their breeding season, and ground-nesting behavior, terns are excellent subjects for study and have been actively managed for many years. Many tern species have a federal or state conservation designation, classifying them as Species of Special Concern, Threatened, or Endangered. Management actions include protecting breeding colonies, controlling human-subsidized predators, educating the public about the threats facing terns, and conducting scientific research and monitoring to gauge population trends. This research often includes efforts to band terns in order to track movements with metal or colored plastic bands, or even with high-tech geolocator devices, which help identify each individual tern. Banding efforts have informed researchers about tern movements, foraging locations, important wintering grounds, and individual causes of mortality.

You can assist conservation efforts by removing trash such as fishing line and balloons, respecting posted colony boundaries to reduce disturbance, keeping cats indoors, keeping dogs on leashes near coastal beaches where terns nest, and reporting any issues to the local management agency responsible for tern management. If you see any banded terns, please report them at www.reportband.gov.

## HOW TO USE THIS GUIDE

**MEASUREMENTS** Each account starts with length, wingspan, and weight. The *National Geographic Complete Birds of North America, Third Edition* (2021) served as the source for measurements, and a combination of *Terns of North America and Europe* (1995) and *Birds of the World* (2022) was used for weights. Weight is often difficult to translate to field identification, though significant differences in weight between birds that are fairly similar in measurements will result in differences in flight style, and are therefore worth a brief mention.

**SIZE AND STRUCTURE** Since how a bird is perceived in the field is of greater value for field identification than are linear measurements, this section describes size based on how large the species in question actually appears in the field compared to similar species they might be seen alongside, or particularly familiar species that are similar in size. Because perceived size and structure are often evaluated simultaneously, this section also includes a description of the structure of the species as it appears in the field.

**BEHAVIOR** Any behavioral traits that might be relevant to field identification are briefly described here.

**FLIGHT** This section includes a brief description of flight style, with an emphasis on traits that differ from similar species.

**RANGE** The geographic range is outlined, with a focus on North America, followed by a thumbnail sketch of worldwide distribution.

**CALL** The primary calls are briefly described, and any differences from the calls of similar species are mentioned where confusion is possible. Calls are a highly useful trait for tern identification that are too often neglected. Though

tern vocalizations are an interesting and lengthy subject, this guide will focus on the most basic and essential vocalizations for identification. The full array of tern vocalizations is not addressed, as each species of tern has a tremendous vocal repertoire, particularly in the immediate vicinity of the nesting colony. Much of a tern's repertoire consists of variations on the primary calls, and so by learning the basic calls, you can often infer the species involved when hearing an unfamiliar vocalization.

**SPECIES INFO** Any piece of information deemed relevant that does not fit neatly into another section is addressed here. Information on subspecies is the most frequent subject, always at the end of the section, but particularly notable life history traits and conservation status may also be included.

**PLUMAGE INFO** This section describes what plumages are most likely to be observed while in North America. Given that some species of terns vacate North America for months at a time, and immature birds often do not return to the breeding ground, it is worthwhile knowing what plumages you are most likely to encounter and when.

**PHOTOS** Photos should speak for themselves, but they can also be misleading. Great care was taken to choose photos that speak most clearly and represent the species depicted as an observer would see them in the field. When available, comparison photos were used to ignite and solidify learning. Because terns are particularly beautiful birds, where possible, photos were chosen that best display that beauty while still being educational.

**PHOTO CAPTIONS** The age and plumage for the species covered in the account are mentioned first, along with the identification of other birds in the image that add context. If the bird depicted is clearly in the midst of a molt, then the symbol ">" will be used to highlight the transition from one plumage to the next. For example, "basic > alt." indicates that the bird is in the midst of the molt from basic plumage to alternate plumage. The month and location of the photo are listed next, followed by the photographer. If no photographer is listed, the image is by the author. The bulk of the caption text is merely an attempt to amplify the voice of the image. Occasionally, there will be quiz captions, with answers located at the back of the book.

**INTRO 14** Common Tern. July, NY. Cathy Sheeter.

# SPECIES ACCOUNTS

Sandwich Tern.

# LARGE TERNS: GENUS *HYDROPROGNE*

**The word *Hydroprogne* is a combination of the ancient Greek word for "water" and the Latin word for "swallow," hence "water swallow." The genus *Hydroprogne* is monotypic, with Caspian Tern being the only species. Caspian Tern is the largest tern in the world, larger even than some medium-sized gulls like Ring-billed Gull. A primarily freshwater species, it makes spectacular plunge-dives, fully submerging its body, to acquire fish.**

## CASPIAN TERN *Hydroprogne caspia*

L 20–22 in.; WS 46–51 in.; WT 18–24.5 oz.

**SIZE AND STRUCTURE** The largest tern in the world, Caspian Tern is distinctly larger than Royal Tern. It is slightly larger than Ring-billed Gull but smaller than Herring Gull, though Caspian Tern projects bulk in a way that almost gives it the bearing of a large gull. The bulk and the huge, deep-based bill dominate first impressions of this species. Caspian Terns are large and bulky with disproportionally small, square heads, and short, slightly forked tails. In flight, the large, wicked-looking bill still dominates the impression of the species, and Caspian Tern points its bill straight down when foraging, thus appearing to be constantly looking downward. Its bill combines with a fairly long, thick neck and short tail to create an imbalanced, front-heavy impression with an almost abnormally short rear. Caspian Tern's body is bulky and is typically broadest right where the leading edge of the wing joins the body, creating a chest-heavy impression that enhances the powerful impression of the bird. In some individuals, though, the body is broadest where the trailing edge of the wing and body join, which still makes them look powerful but also paunchy. The wings are so broad-based that they give the impression of a large gull, but they are swept back sharply at the wrist and taper to a sharp point in a manner that could only belong to a tern.

**BEHAVIOR** Typically flies high for a tern, above eye level most of the time. Often roosts in large, single-species flocks. Sometimes joins Ring-billed Gull roosts in inland locations, or groups of Royal Terns coastally, but typically forages alone or occasionally in pairs.

**FLIGHT** Wingbeats are extremely slow, particularly when foraging, when it often swoops and wheels with an exaggerated grace on deep wingbeats. In migratory flight, Caspian Terns are quite different, maintaining a steady height and speed on wingbeats that, while still slow, are steady and fairly shallow with a uniform, businesslike quality. Migrants often follow rivers or coastlines, moving diurnally in ones and twos, each following the other along a nearly identical path through the air in a consistent steady trickle. Large groups flying together are unusual at most locations.

**CALL** Adults give a loud, far-carrying *Kee-YOW*, often singly with distinct pauses between calls, while juveniles have an incessant, whiny series of peeping calls.

CASPIAN TERN 1 Breeding (alt.) adults. July, NY. Brian L. Sullivan. Bulkier and more powerful than all other terns to such a degree that other ID traits are rendered almost moot. The deep-based bill has a uniquely lethal appearance, and the body has a more gull-like carriage than any other tern. Caspian Tern has a thick neck but a surprisingly small head with a flat-crowned, blocky shape. Most individuals show a dark smudge near the tip of the bill, a trait often cited to separate them from Royal Terns, but some, particularly in late summer and fall, lack the smudge, or show it only faintly.

CASPIAN TERN 2 Nonbreeding (basic) adults with Black Skimmer, Royal Tern, Forster's Tern, and Laughing Gull. Nov., FL. So unique structurally with the broad, dangerous-appearing bill, flat crown, head that is surprisingly small in relation to the rest of the bird's proportions, and massive body that few plumage details even matter. Notice, though, that the finely streaked head is the exact same shape as the black cap of breeding plumage, making it the only tern that regularly shows a year-round capped appearance. Note also that most adult Caspian Terns show a black upper surface to the primaries from late summer through midwinter.

CASPIAN TERN 3 Breeding (alt.) adult. Sept., FL. The bill is usually pointed down in flight while foraging, a trait that catches the eye more readily at greater distances. The black undersides of the primaries are a classic field mark for Caspian Tern in flight. This trait is particularly useful as it is visible at great distances. If there is any additional doubt about the identity of this hulking tern, it ends with a glimpse of the bright red bill, which has more in common with a spearhead than the bill of a bird.

**CASPIAN TERN 4** Nonbreeding (basic) adult with Forster's Tern and Ring-billed and Laughing Gulls. Nov., FL. The largest tern in the world, slightly larger than Ring-billed Gulls and significantly larger than all other terns in the region. Particularly in inland locations, Caspian Terns often gather in mixed flocks with Ring-billed Gulls.

**CASPIAN TERN 5** Nonbreeding (basic) adult with Royal Tern. Sept., GA. Note how much darker-headed the Caspian is—the species only rarely shows the bright white forehead and crown that Royal Tern displays for much of the year. Bill color differences between these species are usually obvious, but also note the differences in bill structure, as some are more similar in color. The black upper surface of the primaries is an often-cited identification trait for Royal Tern, but in the late summer and fall, the primaries of Caspian Tern can be just as black.

CASPIAN TERN 6 Juvenile. Sept., TX. Mark W. Lockwood. The head pattern of first-cycle birds is like that of nonbreeding adults, but much darker, with a solid blackish patch behind the eye. The bill is dingy orange to dull red, but always paler than that of adults. The scalloping on the back is lost quickly, usually beginning in September or October. Unlike juvenile Royal Tern, the tertials are barred rather than having solid dark centers and are held until at least early winter.

CASPIAN TERN 7 Immature with Royal Terns. Oct., GA. Some Caspian Terns lack the dark smudge on the bill tip or show it very minimally. The odd pattern of feather wear in the coverts suggests that this bird is not a full adult, though it looks much like an adult that is just beginning the molt to nonbreeding. *Find the two Caspian Terns in the background—what are their ages?*

**RANGE** **North America:** The breeding range is extensive but so disjunct as to almost seem arbitrary. There is a breeding population in the Gulf Coast and southern Atlantic region; a mid-Atlantic population; populations in a handful of locations in the Canadian Atlantic Provinces; populations throughout the Great Lakes; a large population in the northern Canadian Prairie Provinces; a scattering of small breeding areas throughout the Dakotas, Montana, Idaho, and the northern Great Basin; several disjunct breeding areas in California; a large population centered on the lower Columbia River in Oregon and Washington extending through the Puget Sound to extreme southwestern British Columbia; and, finally, a small population in southeastern Alaska. The species winters primarily in Mexico and the Caribbean but is common along the Gulf Coast and southern Atlantic and well as southern California within the U.S. It is widespread as a migrant, using rivers and coastlines like migratory pathways to connect to its disjointed breeding areas. **World:** Widespread but highly fragmented distribution in Europe, Africa, Asia, and Australia/New Zealand.

CAPIAN TERN 8 First-cycle upper and underwing. Sept., GA. First-cycle birds are darker-headed than nonbreeding adults and almost look like breeding adults but have duller bills. The fine barring on the tail and the faint secondary bar are additional traits that age this bird. The gray hand and secondary bar will gradually darken throughout the winter.

**SPECIES INFO** Found in both fresh and saltwater but most at home in freshwater habitats. Unlike the semi-pelagic crested terns, Caspian Tern restricts its movements and foraging to near-shore waters, usually foraging within easy sight of land. There are no described subspecies.

**PLUMAGE INFO** Because the species is present year-round somewhere in North America in good numbers, all plumages can be readily seen. However, surprisingly for such a large species, the plumage doesn't vary greatly either seasonally or by age.

CASPIAN TERN 9 Nonbreeding (basic) adult with Sandwich Terns and Laughing Gulls. Nov., TX. Dwarfs the Laughing Gulls and the Sandwich Terns. Note the powerful chest, flat crown, and that glowing red, wicked-looking bill.

**CASPIAN TERN 10** Breeding (alt.) adult and juvenile with Royal Terns, Black Skimmers, and Laughing Gulls. Oct., GA. Juveniles follow the adults for months, begging to be fed and uttering an ear-splitting warbling squeal, completely unlike the calls of adults, with amazing repetitiveness. Note that the head pattern of the immature bird is very similar to that of the breeding adult, although the cap is blackish instead of fully black, and the bill is duller.

**CASPIAN TERN 11** Immature, nonbreeding (basic) adult with Royal and Forster's Terns. Nov., TX. While flight feathers are molting, the dark undersides to the primaries are partially obscured for a month or more. The bird in flight could be in the process of completing its preformative molt from the year before, making it just over a year old, as adults are not molting outer primaries in November. The perched adult in the background has the palest crown you are likely to see on a nonbreeding Caspian, but on bulk and bearing alone, it pops out of the group.

**CASPIAN TERN 12** Breeding (alt.) adult. July, NY. Brian L. Sullivan. The wings, particularly their breadth, are strikingly gull-like, until reaching the distinctly tern-like pointed wingtip. This is another individual that lacks the dark smudge near the bill tip, and the bill color on this bird is a bit more like that of a Royal Tern as well. The slow, gull-like wingbeat, the short tail, and the long neck should eliminate any desire to base identification on whether or not a dark bill smudge is present.

**CASPIAN TERN 13** Nonbreeding (basic) adults and first-cycle with Royal Tern. Sept., NJ. Kevin T. Karlson. Royal Terns are big, but Caspian Terns are BIG. The bird standing in the background retains some juvenile plumage, and note how its bill color is quite close to that of the adult Royal Tern. Caspian Terns do not show as much variation in bill color as Royal Terns do, but they show some, and first-cycle birds always have a bill that tends toward orange rather than red.

**CASPIAN TERN 14** Juvenile with Ring-billed Gull. Aug., MD. Daniel Irons. This is a hefty bird! Compare its size to that of the bird of the Ring-billed Gull. The markings on the juvenile feathers on the mantle have faded but are still obvious, and the bird has the dull orange bill typical of first-cycle Caspian Terns.

# CRESTED TERNS: GENUS *THALASSEUS*

**The word *Thalasseus* is a reworking of the ancient Greek word for "sea" while also a reference to a Greek goddess of the sea, Thalassa. Worldwide there are seven species in the genus, three of which occur in North America. These are coastal birds with a showy, all-eyes-on-me demeanor. They are noisy and gregarious, and their breeding displays the stage presence of a Broadway lead. Terns in the genus *Thalasseus* are more prone than most terns to hybridize, but seem to do so only within *Thalasseus*, and in most cases hybridization is brought about by vagrancy.**

## ROYAL TERN *Thalasseus maximus*

L 17–19 in.; WS 41–45 in.; WT 14–17 oz.

**SIZE AND STRUCTURE** The largest of the crested terns and noticeably larger than all terns except Caspian, Royal Tern is slightly smaller than Caspian Tern but with a significantly slimmer build, which results in an even smaller appearance, relative to Caspian, than measurements imply. The sleek, lean structure is set off by a moderately heavy bill and slightly crested head. In flight, the body has an even, tubular shape with a nearly flat belly and medium-length forked tail. The wings are centered on the body, are of even width, and are swept back sharply at the wrist, giving them an angular appearance. Unlike that of Sandwich and, especially, Caspian, its bill is nearly always pointed straight ahead while in flight.

**BEHAVIOR** Essentially a coastal tern, within Royal Tern's range, it is normal to see singles and pairs patrolling parallel to the shoreline a few hundred feet off the beach. However, individuals or groups also forage in pelagic waters far from shore, particularly when feeding young. The species typically breeds in massive colonies, with juveniles gathered together in tightly packed groups, called "crèches," of dozens or hundreds, while adults forage to bring food back to their own youngsters in the crèche.

**FLIGHT** Wingbeats are smooth and powerful with an easy grace and moderate depth. Royals fly fairly high, and often quite quickly for a tern when foraging, and will check suddenly from a straight course, pivot, and dive almost simultaneously, going after prey just passed over, completely unlike the broad wheeling changes of direction favored by Caspian Tern. Individuals may also pull up and hover before making short, direct dives.

**CALL** A loud, rolling *Ker-rrriCCC* that cuts through the air with a ringing quality, sometimes with a short *rik* call interspersed with the longer calls. Juveniles give a shrill, high-pitched squeal that breaks like a teenager's voice. This call is given well into winter and occasionally into the following spring.

ROYAL TERN 1 Breeding (alt.) adult. March, FL. A powerfully built, Ring-billed Gull–sized tern with a modest crest and solid orange bill. The full black cap is held only briefly, usually from March to May in the East, from February to June less regularly, and very rarely later in the year. Royal Terns in California may acquire the full black cap much earlier in the year, rarely as early as December. The primaries are pale gray from early winter but darken gradually during spring and summer, and are often fully black in the fall.

ROYAL TERN 2 Breeding (alt.) adults with Sandwich Tern, Laughing Gull, and Sanderling. April, TX. Laughing Gulls are often found side by side with Royal Terns and are similar in size, so using Laughing Gulls to gauge the size of distant terns is useful. The Sandwich Tern is strikingly similar in silhouette, but distinctly smaller and slimmer-billed than the Royal Terns.

ROYAL TERN 3 Breeding (alt.) adults. May, FL. While most terns have impressive breeding displays, the displays of the crested terns are particularly spectacular, and Royal Terns are a standout even among crested terns. A constant barrage of their noisy, rolling calls accompanies every stage of their spectacular nuptial dance and flight display.

**RANGE North America:** Royal Tern is a year-round resident of the Gulf Coast and the southern Atlantic coast north to North Carolina as well as southern California. Along the Atlantic coast, Royal Tern breeds north to Chesapeake Bay and occasionally to southern New Jersey. Stragglers are found north of their breeding range, north to New England, rarely Atlantic Canada, throughout the summer, disappearing by late September. However, a much larger dispersal of post-breeding adults north along the Atlantic coast to New York and southern New England, many with juveniles in tow, is a regular late summer feature, with individuals remaining in numbers throughout the fall and into the early winter. While small numbers nest in southern California, most are birds that have dispersed north from the major breeding areas in northwestern Mexico. While the species can be relatively common in southern California, it reaches central California very rarely. **World:** Widespread coastally in Central America, the Caribbean, and northern and eastern South America.

**ROYAL TERN 4** Breeding (alt.) adults. March, TX. Kevin T. Karlson. Note the variation in bill color in this image, from dull orange to very reddish. At the height of courtship, some adults briefly show bills that are as red as Caspian Tern and can cause confusion for those that use bill color as a primary identification trait. Note, however, that the size and structure of all the individuals in this flock are identical.

**ROYAL TERN 5** Breeding (alt.) adult. April, TX. In spring, some Royal Terns show a hint of a dark wedge in the primaries, such as here, while others appear to have uniformly pale gray primaries. Some field guides portray a uniformly pale upper wing as a Caspian Tern trait. However, a completely pale upper wing indicates a Caspian Tern only in midsummer and fall, when most Royal Terns show a distinct dark wedge. Likewise, the presence of a dark wedge in the spring is a useful trait for identifying a Royal Tern, but is not useful in the fall, as many Caspian Terns also show a dark wedge on the upper surface of the wing when the outer primaries are worn.

**ROYAL TERN 6** Nonbreeding (chick-feeding plumage) adult. July, TX. Briefly in midsummer, adults hold a highly variable crown pattern intermediate between breeding and nonbreeding. It is theorized that the variety of head patterns shown during this period gives chicks a feature to visually identify their parents.

**ROYAL TERN 7** Juvenile with Elegant Terns. Sept., CA. Full juvenile plumage is held only a few months. The pattern and intensity of dark marks on the back and wings vary greatly. The pale orange bill is duller than that of nonbreeding adults and remains dull until at least the next spring. The legs are orange in most juveniles, but become largely black by the end of September, though splotches of orange can be retained later and may sometimes be present on some adults.

**ROYAL TERN 8** Juvenile, first-cycle, nonbreeding (basic). Sept., GA. Juvenile (center) displays typical begging posture. The dark markings on the back and wing coverts have faded significantly since fledging, but it is still entirely in juvenile plumage (or nearly so). In contrast, the bird on the right is at the midpoint between the appearance of a juvenile and that of first-cycle birds in the winter—the adult-like gray back, messy appearance to the coverts, and dark tertials are all typical of first-cycle Royal Terns. The legs are transitioning from orange to black on both. Both adults (left and center back) are essentially in nonbreeding plumage but have yet to replace their outer primaries, which are worn and dark. Over the course of the winter these primaries will be replaced by fresh, pale gray feathers.

ROYAL TERN 9 First-cycle. Oct., NJ. The first-cycle wing pattern is distinctive, with an entirely dark hand, appearing black at a distance, connecting to an obvious strong dark secondary bar. First-cycle Royals are the only North American terns that show this pattern, and the dark hand can be seen from greater distances than virtually any other identification trait, allowing simultaneous identification and aging of these birds in flight, even when they are mere specks. By midwinter, fresh inner primaries break up the solidly dark hand and create a pattern more similar to first-cycle Elegant Tern.

ROYAL TERN 10 Nonbreeding (basic) adult with Sanderling, Black Skimmer, and Herring Gull. Nov., GA. The nonbreeding head pattern is quite variable, but the central crown and forehead are always largely unmarked, and the eye is usually clearly isolated, unlike Elegant Tern. The bill is usually duller than during the hormonal spike in the spring, but there is still clear variation in bill color, apparent on these individuals. The color of primaries is also variable, from pale, almost uniform with the back on birds with fresh primaries, to blackish on birds that have yet to replace old outer primaries.

**ROYAL TERN 11** Immature (second-winter type). Sept., GA. In flight, Royal Terns are distinctly large and powerful, while still appearing lean and aerodynamic. When foraging, Royal Tern keeps the bill pointed straight forward, while Caspian Tern usually angles the bill downward. Much like Common Terns, Royal Terns show a distinct dark wedge in summer and early fall, while some Caspian Terns also show a dark wedge on the upper side of the wing at this time of year.

ROYAL TERN 12 Nonbreeding (basic) adults with Elegant Terns. Sept., CA. Like the way Greater and Lesser Yellowlegs can be confusing at times when seen individually, but are utterly distinctive in direct comparison, so it is with Royal and Elegant Terns. In this image, the Elegant Tern on the right appears to have a darker gray back. However, back color of the North American crested terns is extremely similar, so that any apparent color difference is just as likely to be due to slight differences in the angle of view as it is to represent actual color differences; overall, back color is an unreliable ID trait in this group.

ROYAL TERN 13 Nonbreeding (basic) adult with Sandwich and Forster's Terns. Nov., TX. Here with several Sandwich Terns and a single Forster's Tern, the greater body mass of the Royal Terns is as distinctive as their glowing orange bills.

**ROYAL TERN 14** Nonbreeding (basic) with Caspian Tern. Sept., GA. The Caspian Tern in the background shows a deeper-based bill with a dark smudge at the tip and a blockier head. Caspians also maintain the heavily streaked head throughout the nonbreeding season, while for much of the year Royal Terns have a predominantly white head, a difference visible at great distances. *What age is the Caspian Tern?*

**ROYAL TERN 15** Nonbreeding (basic) adults and first-cycle with Common Tern and Sanderling. Sept., GA. In fall the folded primaries are black, while in spring the folded primaries are much paler, nearly uniform in color with the birds' gray backs. The Common Tern in the center provides an ideal size comparison. First-cycle birds continue to beg for months after fledging, both on the ground and in flight, ceaselessly uttering their shrill squeals.

ROYAL TERN 16 Nonbreeding (basic) adult with Sandwich Tern. Sept., GA. These two crested tern species overlap in both range and habitat and often gather together at roost locations. They are easily distinguished at all but the most extreme distances.

**SPECIES INFO** Numerous and noisy, Royal Terns seem almost ubiquitous along many warm-water beaches. Royal Tern is among the most likely species to be pushed inland in the wake of tropical systems. While it is currently considered monotypic, the population in southern South America breeds at a completely different time period than the more northerly population; the two likely never come in contact and could represent different subspecies. Until recently *Thalasseus* terns in West Africa were considered a subspecies of Royal Tern, but further examination proved them to be a separate species, West African Crested Tern.

**PLUMAGE INFO** As with all crested terns, it holds its full black cap for only a short period, usually March to May, or February to June for some in the East. In the West, Royal Terns can acquire full black caps as early as late December. As individual Royal Tern lose their cap, they briefly hold a variable "chick-feeding plumage," with irregular black-and-white checkering on the crown. Some have theorized that this varies the appearance of individual adults, making it easier for chicks to identify their parents. Immature birds can be quite variable, but every description of immature birds is usually available to be studied at any large gathering of the species.

## ELEGANT TERN *Thalasseus elegans*

L 14.5–16 in.; WS 37–39.5 in.; WT 7–11 oz.

**SIZE AND STRUCTURE** Slightly larger than Sandwich Tern and distinctly smaller than Royal Tern. Within North America, no other crested tern has such a luxuriant and conspicuous crest. Even in nonbreeding plumage, when other crested terns have muted crests, the crest of Elegant Tern cannot be missed—it is visible as a messy clump of black feathers on the nape even when pressed close to the head. The bill is also notable within this group, the proportionally longest of the North American crested terns—fairly deep at the base, but rapidly tapering to a particularly sharp, dagger-like tip, and showing a slight curve to the upper mandible. In flight, Elegant Tern shows slim wings, but overall manages to appear more like a cut-down Royal Tern than the painfully slender appearance of Sandwich Tern (that it is actually closer to in size).

**BEHAVIOR** Primarily coastal. Like all crested terns, will range far out into the ocean when foraging and also when migrating. Mixes readily with flocks of Royal Terns. Juveniles often follow adults during the post-breeding dispersal in California and beg from adults throughout the summer and fall.

**FLIGHT** Combines the quick wingbeats of Sandwich Tern with the smooth, athletic flight style of Royal Tern. Differences from Royal Tern in flight can be detected when you look for them, but this tends to require a moment or two of judging the speed of the wingbeats and looking at the width of the wings. If done flippantly, without proper consideration, it can be easy to misidentify them, particularly at a distance. This is unlike distinguishing Royal from Sandwich Tern in flight, which is usually nearly instantaneous, thus highlighting how much more similar Elegant Tern is to Royal Tern than Sandwich Tern is to Royal Tern.

**CALL** A quick *kerik-RIK*, very much like Sandwich Tern, but deeper and slightly slower, with less of the scratchy quality. The tone of the call has slight elements that are reminiscent of Royal Tern, although the tone and pattern are extremely close to those of Sandwich Tern.

**RANGE** Present in southern California for much of the year, breeding in several locations. Generally, returns in March and

ELEGANT TERN 1 Nonbreeding (basic) adults. Sept., CA. The crest of Elegant Tern is more dramatic than that of any other North American crested tern. It is unmistakable when raised, but even when held close to the head, it is difficult to conceal, and looks like a black cowlick on the nape. The typical bill color is an orange or reddish-orange base fading distinctly along the outer third. There is a tremendous amount of variability apparent in bill coloration, and birds with more yellowish-based bills show a less noticeable two-toned appearance.

**ELEGANT TERN 2** Breeding (alt.) adults. March, CA. Mark Daly Photography. The exceptionally shaggy crest is displayed to best effect during breeding displays. The bill is most richly colored in the early spring, and the two-toned aspect can be particularly apparent, though still quite subtle in some individuals. Breeding displays like this are accompanied by an ear-splitting cacophony of vocalizations, often lengthier and more excited versions of the typical call.

departs from October to November, although rare in late fall and very rare to absent in January and February. Numbers are augmented during the post-breeding period by birds arriving from the primary colony in Mexico as they disperse north, reaching southern British Columbia in some years, although southern Oregon is a more typical northerly limit. Inland records exist for the Salton Sea and Arizona. The migratory route of this species is a bit mind-blowing: northbound dispersal begins in May and peaks in late summer, when large numbers are present in central and northern California, while the most ambitious move into the Pacific Northwest. In September, no matter where it is, an individual will reverse course and move rapidly south to wintering areas along the Pacific coast of South America, with some traveling much of the way down the coast of Chile. Over the course of the year, many individuals traverse a huge portion of the Pacific coast of the Americas, potentially flying nearly 17,000 miles! **World:** Pacific coast from Mexico to central Chile.

**ELEGANT TERN 3** Nonbreeding (basic) adult with Royal Tern. Sept., CA. The differences in size and bill structure between the Elegant Tern (left) and Royal Tern (right) are striking from every angle. The fuller crest and more extensively black head of the Elegant Tern are also obvious. Elegant Terns have a marginally darker mantle color than Royal Terns, but the difference is not always evident, particularly in strong sun.

**ELEGANT TERN 4** Nonbreeding (basic) adults. Sept., CA. The bill color of Elegant Terns varies greatly: orange- or red-based bills are more typical of adults, while more uniform yellow bills are more characteristic of immature birds, and are a bit more similar to the bills of Royal Tern, while some adults also have a fairly uniform pale orange bill. When attempting to age crested terns, dark-centered tertials (which can faintly be seen on the second bird back) are typically an indication of immature plumage, but occasionally, adults will show the feature faintly. If a crested tern with dark-centered tertials has primary coloration and wear that is similar to other nearby adults, then it is likely an adult; if these traits differ noticeably, it is probably an immature bird.

**ELEGANT TERN 5** Breeding (alt.) adult. May, CA. Brian L. Sullivan. The wings of Elegant Terns are slightly slimmer than those of Royal Terns, and the tails are slightly longer. The slender bill has a slightly decurved shape that is often more noticeable in flight; it is the only North American crested tern with a decurved bill. The narrow secondary bar is a trait shared with some adult Royal Terns.

**ELEGANT TERN 6** Nonbreeding (basic) adult and first-cycle. Sept., CA. The thick crest and extensive black on the head are typical of nonbreeding adults. This black coloring extends forward almost to the midpoint of the crown, nearly above the eye, with far more black on the head than either nonbreeding Royal or Sandwich Tern displays, though the most white-headed Elegant Terns overlap slightly with the darkest-headed Royal Terns. The bill is long, slender, and faintly decurved, with a slight gonydeal expansion just short of the midpoint. Note that the first-cycle bird to the left has a shorter bill that lacks the distinct shape of adult Elegant Terns. In crested terns, it takes months for the bill to reach its full length and shape.

**ELEGANT TERN 7** Nonbreeding (basic) adult with Royal Tern. Sept., CA. The tremendous variability crested terns show in the amount of black in the outer primaries obscures any differences in wing pattern between Royal and Elegant Terns. Elegant Tern does tend to show a larger, more obvious, translucent inner-primary window. Elegant Tern's typical flight call, much shorter than that of Royal and lacking the rolling quality, is one of the best ways to identify it in flight, along with its faster, snappier wingbeat. Also note the distribution of black on the head in relation to the eye.

**ELEGANT TERN 8** Nonbreeding (basic) adult with Royal Tern. Sept., CA. In direct comparison, there is no comparison, though at times Elegant Terns can hide in tightly packed flocks of Royal Terns. While size and bill structure render most other distinctions moot, note how the bill color fades from orange to yellowish on the Elegant Tern, versus the more uniform bill on the Royal Tern, and how the entire top of the head is white on the Royal Tern compared to the mostly black-capped Elegant Tern. Elegant Tern shows particularly evident sexual dimorphism in bill length and shape, with males being longer-billed and showing the more "classic" Elegant Tern shape. This bird appears short-billed, with a bill shape more reminiscent of a small Royal Tern, and so it is likely a female.

**ELEGANT TERN 9** Immature (likely second-cycle). Sept., CA. The decurved bill of Elegant Tern is often more noticeable in flight than when on the ground. While most North American crested terns have a dark wedge in the outer primaries in the late summer and fall, the situation with Elegant Tern is more complex. Due to their lengthy migration to South America, adult Elegant Terns in fall often show a narrow dark wedge three-quarters of the way along the primaries, while the surrounding inner and outermost primaries are contrastingly pale. The pattern shown by this individual, which would be typical of a fall adult Royal Tern, indicates an immature Elegant Tern, while an adult Elegant Tern would have pale outermost primaries and dark central primaries.

**ELEGANT TERN 10** First-cycle (left) compared with first-cycle Royal Tern (right). Sept., CA/Oct., NJ. Notice the pale inner-primary window on the Elegant Tern that breaks up the dark trailing edge, as opposed to the entirely dark hand and continuously dark trailing edge of the Royal Tern. This trait is most useful in fall, as by midwinter, some worn immature Elegant Terns can show a pattern similar to a fall Royal, while as Royal Terns begin to replace inner primaries, the new pale feathers break up the dark trailing edge, creating a pattern similar to immature Elegant Terns. Adult Elegant Terns also show a translucent inner-primary window that adult Royal Terns lack, but the distinction is much more obvious on first-cycle individuals.

**ELEGANT TERN 11** Breeding (alt.) adult. March, CA. Tom Ford-Hutchinson. The crest is irrepressible! Like Sandwich Tern, Elegant Tern individuals can have a faint pink blush on the underparts that varies year to year depending on the food resources available. Adult Elegant Terns are also more prone than other crested terns to show colorful blotches on their black legs, although all crested tern species show this trait occasionally.

**ELEGANT TERN 12** First-cycle. Sept., CA. Recently fledged individuals have pale gray primaries, but the outer primaries quickly wear until they are dark. Like those of any recently fledged tern, the primaries are not yet full length, altering the appearance to a more rounded wing profile. The bill is also not fully grown and is shorter and thicker than that of an older bird.

ELEGANT TERN 13 Nonbreeding (basic) adult with a Sandwich Tern. Nov., Peru. Elegant Tern is slightly, but noticeably, larger than Sandwich Tern, and the difference in the length of the bill in these two individuals is dramatic, though the length of the bill in the shortest-billed female Elegant Terns is more comparable to that of Sandwich Terns.

**SPECIES INFO** In addition to its lengthy multisegmented migratory movements, Elegant Tern is also notable in that roughly 90% of the global population breeds in a single location: Isla Rasa in the Gulf of California. This reliance on a single primary breeding site does represent a distinct risk, as any disaster or ecological changes on Isla Rasa could devastate the species. Interestingly, beginning in about the year 2000, a tiny but growing number of Elegant Terns has turned up in Sandwich Tern colonies in western Europe every year, pairing sometimes with other vagrant Elegant Terns and sometimes with Eurasian Sandwich Terns. They have been found rarely in the eastern U.S. as well, and there is one record of hybridization with Sandwich Tern (in Florida). There are also records of Elegant x Sandwich Tern hybrids in southern California, and some birds breeding at Isla Rasa show traits that indicate hybridization may have occurred there as well.

ELEGANT TERN 14 Juvenile. July, CA. Marquette Mutchler. Lacking a size comparison, this juvenile Elegant Tern has very few traits that separate it from a juvenile Royal Tern. Note particularly that this bird has an almost entirely white crown like a Royal Tern. The two inner primaries are pale gray, though—a useful trait to separate first-cycle Elegant and Royal Terns in the fall.

**ELEGANT TERN 15** Adults with Heermann's Gulls. Aug., CA. Jerry Ting. The variability Elegant Terns show in bill coloration and shape is tremendous. Notice that several have bills that are mostly orange or yellow-orange, and the two-toned effect is quite subtle. Also, some have bills that are shorter and not as curved (females), which makes them appear slightly thicker. These traits serve to make such individuals less distinct from Royal Terns than might be expected. As both species are often seen together in southern California and are easily separated, if careful attention is paid, the variability can easily be downplayed. But what about a vagrant Elegant Tern or an individual seen on its own with no comparison? These beasts vary greatly and the next one you encounter may not be "classic."

**ELEGANT TERN 16** Juvenile and adults. Sept., CA. With adults to compare it to, it is easy to identify this worn juvenile Elegant Tern. But note the white crown and the bill shape that is still developing and is quite like that of a Royal Tern in shape, if not size.

**PLUMAGE INFO** Like most crested terns, Elegant Tern sports a full black cap for only a short period, arriving on the breeding grounds in March with it already in place and beginning to lose it by May or early June. Many show a rosy blush to the chest, mostly in spring, but some throughout the year. From midsummer onward, adults wear nonbreeding plumage. As juveniles often accompany adults in post-breeding dispersal, juvenile and other immature plumages can be observed far north of the breeding colonies, and not just in the southern California and Gulf of California strongholds.

ELEGANT TERN 17
Juvenile. July, CA. Jerry Ting. Again, without a size comparison, this juvenile Elegant Tern looks essentially identical to a juvenile Royal Tern, particularly as it is extremely pale-headed but has a heavily marked back. On average, juvenile Elegant Terns are less heavily marked than juvenile Royal Terns.

## SANDWICH TERN (NORTH AMERICAN SANDWICH TERN)

*Thalasseus sandvicensis*

L 13.5–14.5 in.; WS 34–36 in.; WT 7.3–10 oz.

**SIZE AND STRUCTURE** Significantly larger than Common Tern and significantly smaller than Royal Tern, about the same size as Gull-billed Tern–a lean tern teetering between elegantly slim and appearing to need a cheeseburger or two. The bill is long and extremely slender, a straight peg stuck on the face. In flight, Sandwich Tern gives a lean but balanced or slightly front-heavy impression, with the slender wings centered on the body and held straighter than those of Royal or Gull-billed Terns.

**BEHAVIOR** Like Royal Tern, it sometimes forages well offshore, but does not venture quite as far into pelagic waters as Royal Tern. Sandwich Tern is most often seen patrolling back and forth, paralleling the beach within easy binocular view, or loafing on the shore in mixed groups with Royal Terns. These groups of crested terns often seem to have preferred loafing areas, with flocks returning again and again to the same area after being disturbed, despite the specific patch of sand appearing no different from any other. Like Royal Tern, Sandwich Tern also disperses northward coastally after the breeding season. Sandwich Terns disperse in much smaller numbers than do Royal Terns, usually in singles and pairs by the time they reach the northern Mid-Atlantic—sometimes an adult accompanied by a begging juvenile.

**FLIGHT** Wingbeats are strong and quick, noticeably faster than those of Royal Tern, with a slightly jerky quality compared to the smooth and effortless wingbeats of Royal Tern. At a distance, the yellow tip of the bill is often invisible, making the bill appear shorter and heavier in flight or when pointed downward while foraging.

**CALL** Harsh, scratchy *keerikRIK*. The first part is slightly rolling, and the emphasis is on the second syllable, which is higher and clearer. Overall, it lacks the far-carrying quality of the vocalizations of Royal Terns. Both the first and second syllables of the call can be given individually, or strung together in a quick series. The harsh, argumentative quality of the vocalizations means that when large groups are chattering together, the resulting ruckus has the quality of bickering children in a busy schoolyard.

SANDWICH TERN 1 Breeding (alt.) adults. April, TX. A striking, slender crested tern with a slim bill tipped in yellow. Unlike Elegant Tern, the crest is inconspicuous unless flared, as on this pair. Notice the variation in the amount of yellow on the tips of the bills.

**SANDWICH TERN 2** Breeding (alt.) adults with Royal Terns and American Avocets. April, TX. Most frequently in spring (far more rarely at other times of year), some individuals show a light to moderate pink blush on the underparts, adding extra flair to an already beautiful bird. Among crested terns, Elegant Tern also shows this trait but seems to lack the strong seasonality of Sandwich, whereas it is quite rare in Royal Tern and typically faint when present. Of course, Roseate Tern shows a pink flush most consistently, but pink plumage is otherwise extremely rare in other North American terns. The subtle shade of pale pink shown by terns is a color that photos rarely fully render, so expect terns in the field to appear pinker than in photos.

**SANDWICH TERN 3** Breeding (alt.) adults with Royal Terns, Black Skimmer, and Sanderling. April, TX. Sandwich Terns often gather in mixed flocks with other coastal waterbirds, particularly Royal Tern. Such groups provide the perfect opportunity to fix comparative sizes between species in your mind, to note individual variations, to compare vocalizations, and to pick out subtle structural differences, such as how the very straight bill of Sandwich Tern accentuates the flat crown.

**SANDWICH TERN 4** Breeding (alt.) adult. May, FL. The wings are typically held straighter than those of Royal Tern, and are quite narrow and centered on the slim body. Sandwich Tern often tilts its bill downward when foraging, straight down at times, whereas Royal Tern typically holds its bill pointed straight forward.

**SANDWICH TERN 5** Breeding (alt.) adult with Royal, Common, and Forster's Terns; Black Skimmer; Laughing Gulls; American Oystercatcher; and Sanderling. April, TX. Sandwich Tern is intermediate in size between the *Sterna* terns and large species like Royal Tern. When compared to other species, the lean body and angular wings are particularly evident. *How many Common Terns and how many Forster's Terns can you find in this image?*

**RANGE** Sandwich Tern is a year-round resident in most of Florida and the western Gulf Coast, is a breeder on the central Gulf Coast and along the Atlantic coast north to the Chesapeake Bay, and, in post-breeding dispersal, occurs in very small numbers north to Long Island, rarely farther north to Atlantic Canada. Very rare in southern California, where there are multiple records, but these records may pertain only to a few individuals. Has interbred with Elegant Tern there on two known occasions. May be blown inland by tropical storms, though not as frequently as Royal Tern. **World:** Coastally widespread in Europe, Africa, and southwestern Asia (Eurasian Sandwich Tern); the Caribbean and eastern coast of South America (Cayenne Tern); and Mexico, Central America, and northern South America.

**SPECIES INFO** An entirely coastal species, and the only black-billed member of the crested terns. Current North American taxonomy considers Sandwich Tern a single species with three subspecies: *T. s. sandvicensis* of Europe, Africa, and the Middle East; *T. s. acuflavida* breeding in North America; and *T. s. eurygnathus* breeding in the Caribbean and South America. However, the taxonomic position that prevails over most of the world splits nominate *T. s. sandvicensis* from the New World forms and gives the New World forms the name Cabot's Tern, while Eurasian birds retain the common name Sandwich Tern. To make things more complicated, the name Cayenne Tern is frequently given to *T. s. eurygnathus*, which has a completely yellow bill and intergrades with *T. s. acuflavida* where they come in contact in the Caribbean. Some genetic studies have suggested the difference between *T. s. acuflavida* and *T. s. eurygnathus* is not sufficient to warrant an additional split, while other authors have treated Cayenne Tern as its own species. The situation is not yet settled, but the most likely result is that North American Sandwich Tern (Cabot's) will be considered a separate species from Eurasian-distributed Sandwich Tern, while the ultimate treatment of Cayenne Tern is still very clouded.

**PLUMAGE INFO** All plumages are seen frequently. Like other crested terns, Sandwich Tern holds a full black cap only fairly briefly—March to May or June typically, February to July in some. A midsummer molt of the cap results in an individually highly variable "chick-feeding" plumage, a midpoint between the full black cap and the largely white crown. It is hypothesized that the variable black-and-white checkered pattern that results serves to make it easier for chicks, often gathered in crèches, to identify their parents when they return to feed their young.

SANDWICH TERN 6 Nonbreeding (basic) adult. Sept., GA. For most of the year, adults have largely white heads, nearly identical to the head pattern of Royal Tern in nonbreeding plumage. From winter through spring, or until midsummer on some individuals, the primaries are pale gray, matching the gray back, whereas in the fall, the folded primaries are almost entirely blackish.

SANDWICH TERN 7 Nonbreeding (basic) adult. Jan., FL. The only black-billed crested tern, although, particularly in nonbreeding plumage, Sandwich Tern barely lives up to its "crested" name, as the crest is more like an inconspicuous cowlick. Notice how the body compresses laterally in from the shoulder to the belly, so it is almost V-shaped. No other tern of similar size has such a slender body.

**SANDWICH TERN 8** Nonbreeding (basic) adults. Sept., GA. All crested terns show species-specific tendencies in the pattern of black on the head in nonbreeding plumage. These tendencies are further subject to significant individual variation, as shown by these Sandwich Terns. Nonbreeding Sandwich Terns average less black on the head than either nonbreeding Elegant or Royal Terns—significantly less than Elegant but overlapping with some Royal Terns.

**SANDWICH TERN 9** Immature (first-summer type) with Royal Tern. July, FL. While Sandwich Tern approaches Royal Tern in overall length, the differences in bill depth, head size, and body size are obvious at any distance. The primaries on this particular Sandwich Tern are fresh, not worn nor as blackish as adult Sandwich Terns in midsummer (or the Royal Tern behind), and on the opposite wing, you can see that the outermost primary is growing in. This molt timing suggests that this is an immature bird, probably a year old, even though the overall appearance is like that of an adult.

**SANDWICH TERN 10** Juvenile. July, FL. Recently fledged juveniles often have yellow or orange bills and bare parts. Usually these have turned black by the end of August, but some have colored splotches on the legs until October or later, and occasionally adults will also show patches of color on the legs. Note the dark markings on the scapulars and bold dark centers to the tertials.

**SANDWICH TERN 11** Juvenile and adult (chick-feeding plumage) with Royal Tern. July, FL. The speckled crown of the adult is a briefly held appearance called the "chick-feeding plumage" that coincides with the period when juveniles have recently fledged. The plumage and leg color of juvenile Sandwich Terns are identical to those of juvenile Royal Terns (compare the bird behind the adult Sandwich Tern). The bill and leg color on recently fledged birds is orange or yellow, gradually becoming black over the first few months of life.

SANDWICH TERN 12 Nonbreeding (alt.) adults and first-cycle with Black Tern. Aug., FL. The bill shape of the first-cycle bird (the rightmost in the first line of birds, with orange on the bill) is shorter and therefore appears thicker than those of the adults. While the bill of first-cycle birds is usually fully black by September, it takes months for it to develop the shape of an adult bill. Some can show a slight yellow tip as soon as October, though January is more normal, and many first-cycle birds do not develop it until the following spring. Like all first-cycle crested terns, it has extensive dark centers to the tertials, though these fade and are replaced within a few months by fresh tertials with more subtle dark centers.

SANDWICH TERN 13 First-cycle with Royal Tern, Black Skimmer, and Laughing Gull. Sept., GA. The lack of the yellow tip and the shorter, thicker shape give the bill of first-cycle birds an appearance that is somewhat like that of Gull-billed Tern for several months in the fall and early winter, until the bill begins to look more like that of the adult Sandwich Tern. The different pattern of black on the head and the dark-centered tertials are the primary points of separation from Gull-billed at this age.

**SANDWICH TERN 14** Immature (first-cycle > second-cycle). May, FL. Typical of first-spring birds, the outer primaries are retained juvenile feathers, making precise aging of this bird possible. Very similar to a nonbreeding adult, but still lacking the yellow tip to the bill, and with a partial dark secondary bar and obviously worn outer primaries. The complexity of tern molt is apparent on this individual, with what appear to be primaries of three generations: juvenile (P8–10); fresh alternate (P1); and formative 1, with a molt suspension that gives the appearance of an additional generation (P3–4 old F1, P5–6 newer, post molt suspension F1). Many species of terns show similar complexity. Fortunately, in most cases this has little bearing on species identification, but it can be an interesting rabbit hole to fall into.

**SANDWICH TERN 15** Nonbreeding (basic) adults with Royal Terns. Sept., GA. Sandwich Tern is the only crested tern with a black bill. Compare the slender body of the Sandwich Tern to that of the Royal Tern, whose body almost seems to dwarf its head.

# TRICKY *THALASSEUS*

Crested terns of the genus *Thalasseus* tend to be showy, loud, and extremely gregarious birds, and most are easily identified. There are some exceptions, though. They do, for example, show a tendency to hybridize within the genus, or perhaps their hybrids are merely particularly noticeable. A very challenging *Thalasseus* identification is being thrust on North American birders in the wake of the first confirmed Eurasian Sandwich Tern record from Massachusetts in 2013. As these birds are likely to be split in the future from North American Sandwich Terns, the ability and awareness to detect these stealth vagrants will soon be highly useful. To minimize confusion as much as possible with a complicated subject, within this section the terms Eurasian Sandwich Tern (*Thalasseus sandvicensis sandvicensis*) will reference the Old World population. North American Sandwich Tern (*Thalasseus sandvicensis acuflavida*) will refer to North American birds excluding Cayenne Tern. Cayenne Tern (*Thalasseus sandvicensis eurygnathus*) will refer to the yellow-billed population of the southern Caribbean and South America. A further issue, beyond the scope of this guide, is that the Caribbean population of "Cayenne Tern" breeds at a different time of year from the South American "Cayenne Tern," and the differences between these two breeding populations may be greater than currently recognized. Note that some taxonomic authorities are already splitting North American Sandwich Tern, giving it the name Cabot's Tern. The split is not officially recognized in North America, nor is the name Cabot's Tern likely to be adopted here given the prevailing sentiment against eponyms. The name North American Sandwich Tern was chosen for clarity within this guide instead of Cabot's Tern.

## EURASIAN SANDWICH TERN IDENTIFICATION

Separating Eurasian Sandwich Tern from North American Sandwich Tern is extremely challenging, requiring great attention to plumage detail and vocalizations and very careful photo documentation. There is one known record of Eurasian Sandwich Tern from Massachusetts and another highly probable record from Chicago. Given the complexity of identification and the fact that it is not on the radar for most

TRICKY *THALASSEUS* 1 Nonbreeding (basic) adult and juvenile Eurasian Sandwich Terns with Common Terns and a Roseate Tern. Aug., Great Britain. Lukasz M. Pulawski. The barred tertials and strong V-shaped subterminal markings on the back feathers and coverts recall the juvenile plumage of Roseate Tern and are completely distinctive from the juvenile plumage of North American Sandwich Tern. Both the adult and the juvenile show white flecking and fringing on the black marking behind the eye, imparting a distinctive grizzled appearance. Additionally, the adult shows a very restricted yellow tip to the bill typical of Sandwich Tern and a white trailing edge to the folded primaries similar to that of Roseate Tern, that is broader and extends farther along the primaries than that of North American Sandwich Tern.

TRICKY *THALASSEUS* 2 Nonbreeding (basic) adult Eurasian Sandwich Tern. Sept., Poland. Zbigniew Kajzer. Note the small yellow tip to the bill and the grizzled appearance to the dark area behind the eye. The white trailing edge to the primaries has worn away on this bird, so the separation from North American Sandwich Tern is even more challenging with these late summer and fall adults. The bills of Eurasian Sandwich Terns tend to be slightly longer and thinner than those of North American Sandwich Terns. To my eye, those traits are difficult to detect, but I see the bills having slightly more curvature to the upper mandible and tapering more evenly along their length, so they do not have the straight, peg-like appearance of the bill of North American Sandwich Tern.

TRICKY *THALASSEUS* 3 First-cycle Eurasian Sandwich Tern. Sept., Poland. Zbigniew Kajzer. A first-cycle bird might be more likely to occur in North America than a full juvenile. Hopefully such a bird would still retain juvenile tertials, as this bird does. Also note the bold white tips are clearly visible in the inner and middle primaries. First-cycle birds tend to show this strongly bicolored tail, which first-cycle North American Sandwich Terns lack.

birders, there are likely additional occurrences that have been overlooked. The juvenile plumage is quite distinct, with juvenile Eurasian Sandwich Terns having an appearance that is quite similar to juvenile Roseate Terns, while juvenile North American Sandwich Terns are similar to juvenile Royal Terns. Adults are more challenging, and some are likely impossible to separate in the field visually, particularly breeding adults. However, North American Sandwich Terns do differ from Eurasian Sandwich Terns vocally, giving a call that is similar to North American Sandwich Terns but slower and more exaggerated. The traits of nonbreeding Sandwich Terns are visible in the images in this section.

## CAYENNE TERNS AND CAYENNE x CABOT'S TERN INTERGRADES

Cayenne Tern is currently considered a subspecies of Sandwich Tern, occurring in the southern Caribbean and South America. Should Eurasian Sandwich and North American Sandwich Terns be split, Cayenne Tern is likely to be considered a subspecies of North American Sandwich Tern, not its own species, despite the fact that it is more easily separated visually than Eurasian and North American Sandwich Terns are from one another. Further examination of the complex, particularly comparisons of the Caribbean and South American populations of Cayenne Tern, may change this viewpoint. A yellow to pale orange bill is its most distinctive trait, but it is also slightly larger than North American Sandwich Tern, with a larger bill that is often slightly curved. There is an area in the southern Caribbean where North American Sandwich Terns and Cayenne Terns are found together and interbreed, an area known as an "intergrade zone" (not a "hybrid zone," as it is interbreeding between subspecies). Within this area, many birds show intermediate characteristics. Cayenne Tern is of interest to North American birders since vagrant Cayenne Terns have been observed in North America, primarily in Florida but with a few farther-flung records, including a bird in New York.

Perhaps more relevant is the tendency for birds that look identical to North American Sandwich x Cayenne

TRICKY *THALASSEUS* 4 Nonbreeding (basic) adult Cayenne Tern. July, Aruba. The pale eye-ring is a trait seen frequently in Caribbean Cayenne Terns but very rarely in North American Sandwich Terns. The pale forehead with an otherwise complete black cap was observed on multiple Cayenne Terns at this location but is rarely—if ever—shown by North American Sandwich Terns. This suggests that there may be differences in how Cayenne and North American Sandwich Terns replace the head feathers that may be worth additional investigation.

**TRICKY *THALASSEUS* 5** Breeding (alt.) adult Cayenne Tern and Cayenne x North American Sandwich Tern intergrade. July, Aruba. The lead bird is a likely Cayenne x North American Sandwich Tern intergrade while the rear bird is more like a Cayenne Tern, though it does appear to have a black streak on the bill.

**TRICKY *THALASSEUS* 6** Nonbreeding (basic) adult Cayenne Terns, North American Sandwich Tern, Cayenne intergrades, and Common Tern. July, Aruba. A typical flock from the intergrade zone in Aruba. From left to right: North American Sandwich Tern, Cayenne Tern, Common Tern (background), presumed intergrade tern, presumed intergrade tern, and Cayenne Tern. Intergrades are common and highly variable in the southern Caribbean.

Tern intergrades to be observed along the Gulf Coast. The question about such birds is, are they actually Cayenne intergrades, or are they pure North American Sandwich Terns with aberrant bare part coloration? A strike against the idea of them being intergrades is that, according to our present knowledge, the distribution of North American Sandwich Tern-type birds with aberrant bills appears to be too even: they are spread over the entire Gulf region, as prevalent in Texas as they are in Florida. The assumption is that actual vagrants from the southern Caribbean might be expected to be most regular in Florida, and less frequent in areas farther from the intergrade zone. The data that this assumption is based on is far from complete, however, as such birds tend to fly under the radar of most observers. On the other hand, a mark potentially in the favor of these birds being Cayenne intergrades is that many of them are identical in appearance to birds from the known intergrade zone. The reality is that we just don't know enough about these birds yet to be certain whether they are aberrant North American Sandwich Terns or Cayenne intergrades. Documenting the occurrence of such birds over a broad area, noting their traits and molt sequences, and comparing those traits and patterns of occurrence to patterns from the intergrade zone would be key to advancing our knowledge.

## NORTH AMERICAN SANDWICH x ELEGANT TERN HYBRIDS

The *Thalasseus* challenge in southern California and the Baja peninsula involves very small numbers of clear North American Sandwich x Elegant Tern hybrids but also a larger number of birds that appear to be very similar to Elegant

TRICKY *THALASSEUS* 7 Nonbreeding (basic) adult North American Sandwich Tern or North American Sandwich x Cayenne intergrade. Oct., FL. Are birds such as this just aberrant North American Sandwich Terns, or could they be vagrant Cayenne intergrades? *Thalasseus* terns frequently show aberrant leg color—is it such a stretch to believe they could also show odd bill coloration?

**TRICKY *THALASSEUS* 8** Immature North American Sandwich Tern or Cayenne intergrade. July, FL. This bird seems to show an eye-ring like many Cayenne Terns show, but is overall very similar to North American Sandwich Tern.

**TRICKY *THALASSEUS* 9** Breeding (alt.) adult Elegant x North American Sandwich Tern hybrid. March, CA. Tom Ford-Hutchinson. This bird is likely the offspring of a known mixed Elegant Tern and North American Sandwich Tern pair in southern California. Even without that knowledge, it is a clear hybrid, showing its North American Sandwich Tern parentage clearly in the bill, while its shaggy crest screams Elegant Tern.

Terns save for some dark markings on the bills and occasionally other traits that suggest North American Sandwich Tern. In a study of North American Sandwich x Elegant Tern hybrids from the main nesting location for Elegant Terns, Isla Rasa in the Sea of Cortez, these Elegant-like terns were presumed to be backcrosses with Elegant Terns. The researchers used a scoring system to indicate where each bird fell on a scale between pure Elegant and pure North American Sandwich Tern. In their sample of over 1000 birds, those with presumed hybrid traits made up just over 0.5% (Velarde and Rojo 2012). The researchers on this project have obtained blood samples of two such birds, and are working to discover if North American Sandwich Tern genes can be confirmed. Interestingly, birds with dark markings on an orange bill seemed to choose to mate with other birds with the same traits, a tendency also observed in Common x Roseate Tern hybrids (Hays 1975). Others have contended that there are too many of these birds with dark markings on the bill for them to be hybrids, and that they are instead Elegant Terns with aberrant bare part coloration. This is quite similar to the North American Sandwich x Cayenne intergrade versus aberrant North American Sandwich Tern debate in the southeastern U.S. Similarly, there isn't enough data at present to make a determination. There are some banding efforts underway that might shed some light on the problem, but birders in the region are encouraged to carefully document any Elegant Terns with aberrant traits in the hopes that we can use such findings to further our knowledge on the issue.

TRICKY *THALASSEUS* 10 Breeding (alt.) adult presumed Elegant x North American Sandwich Tern backcross (foreground) and Elegant Tern. May, Mexico. Patricia Rojo. This individual from Isla Rasa was one of the individuals considered in a study of presumed Elegant x North American Sandwich Tern hybrids from the Sea of Cortez. In addition to the bill coloration, note the shorter, thinner bill, smaller size, and reduced crest compared to the Elegant Tern in the background. In the study, birds with largely orange bills, but with some traits consistent with Sandwich Terns, were presumed to be backcrosses between an Elegant x North American Sandwich Tern hybrid and an Elegant Tern.

# UPLAND TERNS: GENUS *GELOCHELIDON*

The word *Gelochelidon* is a combination of two ancient Greek words meaning "to laugh" and "swallow," or "laughing swallow." The genus *Gelochelidon* is monotypic, with Gull-billed Tern being the only species, though some taxonomic authorities split the Australian subspecies of Gull-billed Tern into its own species. Behaviorally quite distinct from other terns, it is the tern least tied to water. Gull-billed Tern often forages by flying over dry land in search of grasshoppers and other large insects, frogs, or crabs, which it plucks from the surface, or by catching flying insects midair. It infrequently also forages over water, but its foraging behavior remains the same while doing so: swooping and plucking from the surface, not plunge-diving like most other terns. In most areas this species is somewhat scarce and local, often just a few pairs situated along the edge of a larger colony of terns, except along the Gulf Coast, where it can be locally common.

## GULL-BILLED TERN *Gelochelidon nilotica*

L 13–14 in.; WS 35–38 in.; WT 7–10 oz.

**SIZE AND STRUCTURE** About the same size as Sandwich Tern and slightly larger than Forster's Tern, but distinctly more heavily built than either. The combination of the namesake short, heavy bill with the overall stocky build is structurally unlike any other similarly sized tern. In flight, the wings are unusually broad, while the hand is long and tapered, appearing gently curved at times like the profile of Black Tern, but can also appear very sharp and angular, more like *Thalasseus* terns. The tail is short and only slightly forked. The heavy bill is generally pointed downward, although Gull-billed Terns show more head movement while foraging than any other tern, the bill constantly changing angles as these birds look around.

GULL-BILLED TERN 1 Breeding (alt.) adult. July, FL. The heavy black bill is unique among North American terns. The body is also heavily built, and the legs are long and sturdy. Overall, Gull-billed Tern is fairly plain; while standing, it lacks the elegant appearance that is inherent to most terns. During most of the year, the folded primaries are pale, but in late summer, Gull-billed Terns do show blackish primaries, as this individual does.

GULL-BILLED TERN 2 Breeding (alt.) adults. April, TX. Kevin T. Karlson. Like all terns, Gull-billed Terns engage in an elaborate breeding display to cement the pair bond, and these displays often end with a quick formal bow. Some courtship behavior continues throughout the breeding season, and adults will sometimes bow to each other after feeding chicks.

GULL-BILLED TERN 3 Subadult with Royal Tern, Laughing Gull, American Avocet, and Sanderling. April, TX. The heavy body of Gull-billed Tern makes it appear closer in size to Royal Tern than to Sandwich Tern. While Gull-billed and Sandwich Terns are similar in most measurements, the slim bodies of Sandwich Tern, comparing both species to Royal Tern, highlights how measurements do not capture the full picture of size as it is perceived in the field. The white area at the front of the cap may indicate that this is a second-cycle bird.

**GULL-BILLED TERN 4** Breeding (alt.) adult. April, FL. The broad wings are a noticeable trait in flight, and the head, neck, and body are of nearly equal thickness, so that the entire body looks like a seamless tube. In spring and early summer, the upper sides of the wings of Gull-billed Tern are uniformly silvery-gray, but many develop a dark wedge in the outer primaries as the summer progresses.

**GULL-BILLED TERN 5** First-cycle with Forster's Tern, Common Tern, and Black Skimmer. Sept., LA. Cameron Rutt. This image illustrates how easily photos can mislead. This Gull-billed Tern does not look markedly larger than the *Sterna* terns that surround it, but its body is subtly turned more toward the camera, causing the full breadth of the wings and the bulk of the body to appear diminished. Our eye is drawn, however, to the large, pale head and oddly thick bill, clearly marking this tern as the odd bird out.

**GULL-BILLED TERN 6** Breeding (alt.) adults. July, NJ. George L. Armistead/Hillstar Nature. In contrast to the gregarious nature of most other tern species, Gull-billed Tern does not typically form single-species-dominated flocks. Even in places where they are common, a flock as large as the one pictured here is unusual. More often, singles and pairs tuck themselves into flocks of other terns. Note the heavy bills and dome-shaped heads. *One of these birds differs from the others—which one is in question, and how does it differ?*

**GULL-BILLED TERN 7** Nonbreeding (basic) adult with Forster's Tern. March, FL. Reinhard Geisler. Perched and at a distance, the greater bulk of the Gull-billed is far more noticeable. This individual has only a hint of a dark line behind the eye, and the uniformly pale folded primaries are typical of a fresh-plumaged Gull-billed. *What age is the Forster's?*

**GULL-BILLED TERN 8** Nonbreeding (basic) adult. Feb., FL. Reinhard Geisler. The short, heavy bill and dome-shaped head are distinctive, but in a very subtle way. The head pattern is quite pale, but note the ghost of a dark spot behind and below the eye. Some nonbreeding Gull-billed Terns show a dark eye patch much more clearly, appearing like a dark streak through the eye, extending in front of the eye and tapering off behind it.

**GULL-BILLED TERN 9** Juvenile with juvenile Sandwich Tern and juvenile Laughing Gull. Aug., FL. Fresh juvenile Gull-billed and Sandwich Terns that do not have fully grown bills can be surprisingly similar; the bill structure in particular is much more similar at this age than later in life. The Gull-billed is the front-right bird; note its plain face, dome-shaped head, and plain gray tertial centers compared to the extensive black behind the eye, flat crown, and dark-centered tertials of the juvenile Sandwich Tern.

**GULL-BILLED TERN 10** Breeding (alt.) adult. Aug., GA. While generally silent away from breeding grounds, Gull-billed Tern is extremely vocal anywhere near a nesting area, giving a series of short, bark-like laughs, and an extended chattering cackle. It opens its mouth extremely widely to give these calls; you can identify them at a distance by seeing the mouth open and close before you hear the call.

**GULL-BILLED TERN 11** Breeding (alt.) adult with Sandwich Terns. April, TX. The short, heavy bill and dome-shaped head contrast with the long, slender bills and shaggy crests of the Sandwich Terns in the background.

**GULL-BILLED TERN 12** Juvenile. July, NJ. Kevin T. Karlson. The edges of the back feathers on fresh juveniles are pale brown to bronze, but from a distance, they appear peach-colored or sandy. The lower mandible may show some dull orange or pink until mid-fall, though in most, the bill rapidly becomes entirely black. This individual has a more Forster's Tern-like facial pattern. In Gull-billed Terns with extensive dark around the eye, the pattern consists more of a dark streak through the eye, connecting to a round spot behind it, rather than the more rectangular eye patch of Forster's. Of course, from a distance, the appearance is quite similar.

**BEHAVIOR** Breeds near the coast but often hunts in marshes and upland areas on the coastal plains. When hunting upland areas with high prey concentrations, groups of dozens may gather, coursing and swooping in every direction, unlike groups of terns feeding over water, which usually organize themselves in some discernable way. Along the Atlantic coast, Gull-billeds are usually less numerous than along the Gulf, often nesting on the edges of Common Tern colonies and opportunistically swooping down and snagging Common Tern chicks at unattended nests.

**FLIGHT** Slow, deep, deliberate wingbeats give Gull-billed Tern a beautiful and almost majestic appearance in flight. Individuals generally fly at a medium height above water, mudflats, or open fields, making shallow dives to deftly pluck prey items from the surface, barely arresting their momentum to do so.

**CALL** Usually not particularly vocal except near the breeding colonies, where they are extremely vocal. Typical call is a *Ka-wek* given singly or in a series. The alarm call is an *Aah* given rapidly and repeatedly, becoming a highly unusual cackling laughter. Like juvenile *Thalasseus* terns, the juveniles follow the adults, giving a shrill "peep," though not as frequently or as insistently.

**RANGE** Breeds along the entire Gulf Coast, along the Atlantic coast north to Long Island, and in two colonies in extreme southern California. Generally found in low numbers except for a few locations in Texas and Louisiana. Some individuals winter along the western Gulf Coast and in the Florida peninsula, but generally even scarcer and more local during winter. **World:** Widespread but spottily distributed in Central and South America, southern Europe, Africa, southern Asia, and Australia. Australian birds are split off as "Australian Tern" by some authors.

**SPECIES INFO** The genus name *Gelochelidon* roughly translates to "laughing swallow," in reference to its unusual call and elegant flight. Six subspecies worldwide, with two in North America: *G. n. aranea* in eastern North America and *G. n. vanrossemi* in extreme southern California and the Gulf of California. They are nearly identical, but *vanrossemi* has, on average, a larger bill and longer legs.

GULL-BILLED TERN 13 Juvenile with Black Skimmer and Laughing Gull. Aug., GA. The peach-colored back of a recently fledged Gull-billed Tern fades quickly; by fall, first-cycle birds look quite similar to nonbreeding adults. Note the bulky body, relatively long legs, and upright posture.

**PLUMAGE INFO** Most seen in the United States will be adults in breeding plumage. Immature birds are less apparent than in most other terns. Is that because immature birds stay on the wintering grounds until they are old enough to breed, or are they similar enough to adults that they are not being detected? Wintering Gull-billed Terns are scarce away from a few locations on the coasts of Florida, Texas, and Louisiana. Juveniles can be seen on the breeding grounds, but by fall, first-cycle birds are very similar to nonbreeding adults.

GULL-BILLED TERN 14 Breeding (alt.) adult. July, NJ. Gull-billed Tern forages over dry sandflats, mudflats, openings in coastal marshes, and even grassy fields—habitats rarely used by other terns. Wingbeats are slow and extremely deep, both above and below the body, giving the flight an exaggerated grace that is distinctive and punctuated by shallow, swooping dives as the birds deftly pluck prey, often fiddler crabs, frogs, or large insects, from the surface. Gull-billed Tern's behavior and habitat are such outliers from other terns that these traits can serve as a highly useful "field mark," especially when combined with its size and uniformly pale color.

GULL-BILLED TERN 15 Juvenile. July, CA. James Pawlicki. This faded juvenile already looks much like a nonbreeding adult, but the faint gray marking on the back, and the dark marking on the greater coverts and tertials, make it a clear juvenile. Gull-billed Terns in the West are of the subspecies *G. n. vanrossemi*, and while adults are essentially identical, it is possible that the juvenile plumage differs from that of the eastern subspecies, a pattern seen in several species of terns. Are the strong dark subterminal markings on the tertials and greater coverts due to it being just a particularly well-marked juvenile, or are juvenile western Gull-billed Terns noticeably more heavily marked than those of the eastern subspecies?

# MEDIUM-SIZED TERNS: GENUS *STERNA*

The word "stearn" is an ancient Old English word for "tern," and the Swedish taxonomist Carl Linnaeus reworked it to *Sterna* as the name for the genus. Worldwide, there are sixteen species in the genus, four of which occur in North America. Virtually all terns were at one time placed in *Sterna*, but a reordering of terns in 2005 stripped away most species, leaving only the most stereotypical terns in this genus. The species in North America highlight the diverse life history traits encompassed in *Sterna*, which includes the heralded long-distance migrant Arctic Tern, the short-distance migrant Forster's Tern, the ubiquitous Common Tern, and the scarcely distributed Roseate Tern. The similarity and often overlapping ranges of these four species make them the centerpiece of any tern identification debate.

## FORSTER'S TERN *Sterna forsteri*

L 12.5–14 in. (tail-streamers +2.5);
WS 30–33 in.; WT 5.5–6.8 oz.

**SIZE AND STRUCTURE** The largest of the *Sterna* terns, larger than Common Tern by a slight but noticeable margin; distinctly smaller than Gull-billed and Sandwich Terns. In direct comparison to other *Sterna*, Forster's thicker bill, larger head, slightly heavier body, and longer legs—causing it to clearly stand taller—are noticeable. Without direct comparison, the differences in size and structure will likely be useful only if you have significant experience with Forster's Tern and similar species.

**BEHAVIOR** Frequently perch on posts, docks, and other structures, perhaps as they are often in marsh habitat with limited visibility rather than on open beaches. Foraging behavior very similar to that of Common Tern.

FORSTER'S TERN 1 Breeding (alt.) adult. April, TX. Forster's Terns are usually quite distinctive: they are the largest of the North American *Sterna* terns and have noticeably heavier bills and longer legs than all other *Sterna*. Breeding adults are extremely pale, unlike Common and Arctic Terns, with white or very pale gray chests and bellies. The primaries are a pale silvery-white, distinctly paler than the pale gray mantle. The bright orange legs and base of the bill are exclusive to Forster's among the *Sterna*. During the period when Forster's Terns have black caps, the broad gap between the gape line and cap is a useful trait for distinguishing it from Common Tern.

**FORSTER'S TERN 2** Nonbreeding (basic) adult. Nov., GA. For most of the year, Forster's Tern lacks the full cap but sports this distinctive black eye patch. The silvery primaries are paler than the light gray back, a characteristic Forster's trait. The bright orange legs are also diagnostic. In short, the species is generally easy to identify, particularly in the late fall and winter months, when Forster's are the default *Sterna* in most locations in the U.S. and Canada.

**FORSTER'S TERN 3** Nonbreeding (basic) adult. Nov., TX. In flight, the distinctive eye patch and the entirely silvery primaries remain highly useful distinguishing features. The wingbeats are a tiny bit slower and choppier than those of Common Terns, and the wings are broader than those of all other North American *Sterna* terns. The dark trailing edge to the wing is at the dark extreme on this individual, quite broad but very diffuse. Some Forster's Terns, however, barely show this trait, whereas Common and Arctic Terns always show it clearly.

**FLIGHT** Very similar to Common Tern in point-to-point flight but with marginally longer pauses at the apex and bottom of the wingstroke, creating a slightly jerkier flight impression than that of Common Tern. This difference is slight, but it does create a slightly different impression that can be learned with practice. In high winds, the greater weight of Forster's makes it more stable than Common Tern, but it is slightly less agile and graceful in light winds.

**CALL** Typical call a hoarse *kyarr*, lower-pitched than that of Common Tern's typical call and lacking the dip in pitch that gives the call of Common Tern a two-part quality. Also a hard *tick* that is lower-pitched and fuller than the similar call of Common Tern and is the primary call heard during winter.

**RANGE** Has widespread but spotty breeding distribution in the western Gulf Coast, Mid-Atlantic, Great Lakes, Midwest, prairie potholes region, and Great Basin, and occurs sparsely along the Pacific coast. Post-breeders occasionally stray as far north as Atlantic Canada. The only *Sterna* that regularly winters in North America, along the entire Gulf Coast, the southern Atlantic coast north to the Mid-Atlantic, coastal California, and into the interior along the Mississippi Basin north to Kentucky, and Oklahoma. **World:** Winters in Mexico, Central America, and the Caribbean.

**SPECIES INFO** Primarily a species of freshwater lakes and marshes or coastal backwaters. Forster's Terns can occur on coastal beaches, but in coastal areas they prefer bays, saltmarsh channels, and other protected bodies of water slightly removed from the immediate coast. In winter, some are found on inland reservoirs in the Southeast, particularly those also frequented by Bonaparte's Gulls. This is the only *Sterna* that is almost entirely restricted to North America. Birds breeding in the interior and West are marginally larger with slightly darker gray mantles and chests than those on the East Coast, and are given the subspecific designation *S. f. litoricola* by some authors, though most authorities consider the differences too small for subspecific recognition.

**PLUMAGE INFO** The characteristic black eye patch is a familiar trait for most of the year in most plumages. Adults acquire the complete black cap in late March or early April as part of their molt into breeding plumage, temporarily obscuring the characteristic eye patch. The full cap is lost as early as July (more regularly August), although some retain remnants of it until September. Aside from the period when adults hold the full cap, Forster's Terns of all ages are quite similar, very pale overall with the standout black eye patch. During the molt to breeding plumage in early spring, they go through a brief period when the head pattern mimics a nonbreeding Common Tern. At this time, more care is required to distinguish these species. Another potential confusing period is during the second cycle, when Forster's Terns molt inner primaries but not outer primaries as part of a very early prealternate molt, resulting in pale inner primaries and dark outer primaries, a pattern appearing in winter through the following summer. This pattern closely mimics the typical pattern of adult Common Terns in summer.

FORSTER'S TERN 4 Nonbreeding (basic) adults. Oct., NJ. At a distance, the impression is of an overwhelmingly pale bird with a contrasting black eye patch—a simple, distinctive pattern. Note the body shape of the center bird, expanding notably at the chest, becoming almost perfectly flat across the belly. This structure is unique to Forster's, as both Common and Arctic Terns show slightly rounded bellies, and the ultra-lean Roseate Tern lacks the expansion at the chest. The tail-streamers of all *Sterna* terns often disappear against pale backgrounds, creating a short-tailed impression.

**FORSTER'S TERN 5** Juvenile and breeding (alt.) adult. July, NJ. Juveniles show a solid wash of color across the back, varying individually from dark brown to pale peach, the only juvenile *Sterna* with near-uniformly dark back. This trait is useful for only a short period, though, as by mid-August, most have faded; by October, young of the year have replaced their back feathers with pale gray, adult-like feathers. The diagnostic black eye patch, however, is present throughout the first winter.

**FORSTER'S TERN 6** Juveniles with juvenile Common Tern. Aug., NJ. Kevin T. Karlson. The eye patches give away the two juvenile Forster's flanking the juvenile Common. Also notice the larger head, thicker bill, and longer, thicker legs of the Forster's, as these traits are useful regardless of age or plumage. Much of the back color has faded on the juvenile Forster's on the right, but traces of the unique brown-washed back remain. The blackish shoulder bar on the shoulder of the Common Tern is a trait Forster's Terns never show. Notice the dusky centers to the tertials on the Forster's, a unique trait among juvenile *Sterna* terns, whereas the pale tertials marked with dark subterminal Vs on the Common Tern is the typical pattern among other juvenile *Sterna*.

**FORSTER'S TERN 7** Immature (first-cycle) with Bonaparte's Gulls. Sept., OH. Just a few months out of the nest, this first-cycle Forster's is nearly identical to nonbreeding adults, with the dusky tertials being the most obvious clue to age. The primaries are already darker than the frosty white primaries of adult Forster's and will continue to darken gradually throughout the winter. Note the size compared to Bonaparte's Gull, smaller but not dramatically so. Also note the blocky head shape and heavy bill, which are unlike those of other *Sterna* terns.

**FORSTER'S TERN 8** Immature (first-cycle). Oct., NJ. The dusky tips to the tail feathers, short tail-streamers, and white tips to the greater coverts distinguish this individual from an adult. The brown-washed back seen in juvenile plumage is now entirely replaced with adult-like feathers. The primaries are starting to show dusky tips and will continue to gradually darken until the juvenile primaries are replaced the following summer. The kidney bean–shaped eye patch is the calling card of Forster's, present in most plumages for most of the year.

**FORSTER'S TERN 9** Immature (first-cycle) with immature Common Tern and Laughing Gull. April, TX. Kevin T. Karlson. First-cycle Forster's are the only *Sterna* to show extensively dark-centered tertials, and so that trait both identifies and ages this bird. It is also the only *Sterna* to never show even a hint of a dark shoulder bar, whereas the Common Tern to the right has a prominent shoulder bar. The juvenile primaries have darkened throughout the winter and are now darker than the body. First-cycle Forster's Tern can show very dark or black primaries from late winter through the summer until the juvenile primaries are replaced. Forster's and Common Terns have very different molt strategies. While these birds are both in their first spring, the Common Tern has gone through an extensive molt that included its flight feathers, resulting in the flight feathers appearing fresher and paler than those of the Forster's, while the Forster's has retained juvenile wing coverts, tertials, and flight feathers that are now 8–9 months old. The difference in size is fairly subtle, but hone in on the greater bulk and the larger, blockier head of the Forster's.

**FORSTER'S TERN 10** Breeding (alt.) and molting (basic > alt.) adults with Black Terns and Laughing Gull. April, TX. During the molt from nonbreeding to breeding plumage in early spring, the appearance of Forster's can be bewilderingly variable, and the characteristic eye patch is obscured as individuals acquire the full black cap. Note, however, the orange legs, as Forster's is the only *Sterna* with legs that are clearly orange; all these birds are Forster's except for the little clump of Black Terns to the right. In situations where some of the standard plumage traits are obscured, pick out the most easily identifiable member of the group and compare it to all the others. If the size and structure are identical or nearly so, you can assume all are of the same species. While *Sterna* terns are quite similar, they are not so similar that, in direct comparison, the differences in size and structure between species would be easily overlooked.

**FORSTER'S TERN 11** Immature (first-cycle > second-cycle). July, NJ. This immature Forster's is potentially tricky, as both the head pattern and the black primaries are superficially similar to those of immature Common Terns. Forster's Terns with dark primaries are far more common than is currently recognized. During the late spring and summer, first-cycle individuals, like this bird, often have black primaries, and heavily worn adults in late summer may as well. The long legs are the most obvious Forster's trait in this image. Also note the lack of a carpal bar and the fact that the dark area around the eye is glossy black, rather than the matte black tinged with brown of Common Terns at this age. Forster's with black primaries typically show bold white feather shafts, while the pale feather shafts on Common Terns are narrower and less obvious, if not invisible.

**FORSTER'S TERN 12** Breeding (alt.) adult. April, TX. Orange makes it easy—it's a Forster's! The bright orange legs and bill base are dead giveaways. The long tail projecting well beyond the wingtips and the silvery folded primaries that are even paler than the back are further confirmation of a breeding Forster's. On the Gulf Coast, a pale tern sitting on a post in the middle of a marsh is almost certainly a Forster's or a Gull-billed, even without looking at any other traits. Common Terns prefer to perch on shorelines, not posts. Forster's also tend to show more extensive black on the bill tip than do Common Terns in full breeding plumage. However, due to seasonal variability in bare part coloration in both species, this trait is useful only at the height of the breeding season.

**FORSTER'S TERN 13** Molting (basic > alt.) April, TX. The eye patch continues to stand out on birds in the early stages of the molt to breeding plumage. It is solidly black, compared to the white-flecked crown and nape, and is still somewhat visible, with scrutiny, on birds further into the molt. Notice how clearly the eye patch stands out on the bird in the background despite the dark feathers beginning to fill in the black cap. While the dark flecking on the heads of these individuals is due to the molt to breeding plumage, a small percentage (<1%) of Forster's maintain a similar appearance throughout the winter.

**FORSTER'S TERN 14** Breeding (alt.). adult. July, UT. Forster's Terns with distinct gray chests occur rarely, but are far more regular than is currently recognized. While they can occur anywhere, they are more regular in western North America. There are very few Forster's Terns that have significantly darker underparts than this individual, but such birds are so rare that this may actually be due to a pigment disorder rather than being the extreme end of standard variation.

**FORSTER'S TERN 15** Breeding (alt.) adult. April, Texas. George L. Armistead/ Hillstar Nature. The pattern of fading from the pale gray back and inner wing to the silvery-white primaries, lacking any dark marking on the upper wing, is unique to adult Forster's Terns among *Sterna*. The long tail-streamers are far more rigid than those of Roseate and Arctic Terns, so they do not bounce noticeably with every wingbeat or change of direction. Also note how the white rump stands out, as it is set between the gray back and faintly gray tail, another unique Forster's trait, but one that is better picked up by a camera than in the field.

**FORSTER'S TERN 16** Nonbreeding (basic) adult. Jan., FL. Some Forster's Terns show variable amounts of dark mottling on the crown and nape throughout the winter, some more extensively than that of this individual. By late January, a few Forster's begin to acquire their black cap, increasing the percentage that show a darkish head during the winter. Dark-centered tertials are a known trait in adult *Thalasseus* terns but seem much rarer in Forster's Tern.

## COMMON TERN *Sterna hirundo*

L 11.5–12.5 in. (tail-streamers +1.5);
WS 29.5–32.5 in.; WT 3.8–5.8 oz.

**SIZE AND STRUCTURE** Slightly smaller than Forster's Tern and slightly larger than Arctic and Roseate Terns, but close enough to all three that direct comparisons are usually needed to detect differences. Structurally, it is average in every respect, making it the perfect reference standard for the *Sterna* group. It has a smaller, more rounded head and slimmer bill than Forster's Tern, but a larger bill and larger, less rounded head than Arctic Tern. Overall, Common Tern has balanced proportions and no highly notable structural traits. In flight, the wings are centered on the body. During the breeding season, the species shows the shortest tail-streamers of the *Sterna* group, not extending beyond the folded primaries when at rest. However, these delicate streamers frequently break off, so any *Sterna* can display short streamers.

**BEHAVIOR** Unlike Arctic Tern and Roseate Tern, it often migrates in near-shore waters and along rivers in the interior. These movements can be highly visible, though distinguishing true migration from local movements can still be difficult. Common and Forster's Terns display very similar foraging behavior, establishing the norm for *Sterna* terns. Arctic and Roseate Terns diverge from the norm at times, each in different ways. In order to use the differing foraging strategies of Arctic and Roseate for identification, though, you need to have paid attention to Common Tern's behavior. Common Tern usually makes quick dives at low to moderate distances above the water, diving at a steep angle but not vertically, so they hit the water slightly ahead of where they began the dive.

COMMON TERN 1 Breeding (alt.) adult. July, FL. The defining trait of Common Tern is its lack of distinctive traits, at least when compared to other *Sterna* terns. It has a medium-length bill and legs, it is medium gray, and the bill and leg color is moderately bright red. As it is the most widely distributed member of the *Sterna* group and also the most generic, it is the default reference standard for the rest of the group across much of the continent—all traits are judged in comparison to those of Common Tern. For this reason, it is useful to acquire an intimate familiarity with Common Tern to simplify all *Sterna* identification.

COMMON TERN 2 Nonbreeding (basic) adult with Royal Tern. Sept., GA. Except for the older worn primaries, which will not be replaced until after fall migration, this is nearly full nonbreeding plumage. While some worn Forster's Terns show blackish primaries, most *Sterna* terns with entirely dark primaries are Common Tern. However, not all fall Common Terns have entirely dark primaries—many still show a distinct dark wedge in the fall.

COMMON TERN 3 Breeding (alt.) adult (lower) and immature (second-summer type, upper). Aug., MA. Most Common Terns in summer show a broad dark wedge on the upper wing formed by the 4–5 worn, older outer primaries contrasting with 5–6 paler inner primaries that have been replaced in the spring. It is a highly visible and useful identification trait, as other *Sterna* rarely show such an extensive dark wedge in summer.

COMMON TERN 4 Juvenile. July, NJ. Fresh juveniles are beautiful in an understated way with soft buff on the head, back, and wings. Juveniles of Arctic and Roseate Terns do not show these warm brownish tones to the back. The strong dark shoulder bar is a well-known Common Tern trait and is present on all but breeding adults, though depending on how the feathers are arranged, this feature can be easily hidden.

COMMON TERN 5 Breeding (alt.) adult. Aug., MA. Although the broad, dark trailing edge to the outer primaries is an often-mentioned identification trait, it is actually quite variable and can be difficult to judge. However, when it is shown as strongly as on this individual, it is definitive. The dark outer web to the outermost tail feathers is another frequently mentioned trait (shared with Arctic Tern but differing from Forster's and Roseate Terns), but it is difficult to see, and shadows can cause it to be misinterpreted. The usefulness of this trait (limited) is not in line with the amount of attention it receives in many guides. It tends to only be useful in photos.

COMMON TERN 6 Breeding (alt.) adult with Forster's Tern. July, NJ. The idea that *Sterna* terns are all the same size and nearly identical in structure is easily disproved in direct comparison. Notice the smaller head of the Common Tern, as well as the shorter legs and less bulky body. Also, during the breeding season, Common Terns have reddish legs and base of the bill, compared to the distinctly orange bare parts of Forster's.

COMMON TERN 7 Breeding (alt.) adult. July, NJ. A classic Common Tern, with a strong dark wedge visible on the opposite wing and a broad but defused dark trailing edge visible on the near wing. Also note the structure: the wings are centered on the body with a relatively long neck, long bill, and short tail. Also note that the white wedge between the gape line and black cap is far broader than that of Arctic Tern, yet narrower than that of Forster's Tern.

**COMMON TERN 8** Nonbreeding (basic) and breeding (alt.). Sept., FL. Dan Irizarry. Different appearance, same structure. The bird on the left has worn off virtually all the pale powder that makes the primaries appear light for much of the year. The bird on the right has maintained much more of this pale powder than is typical at this time of the year, though the underlying black is peeking through.

**FLIGHT** Flies strongly with deep, powerful wingbeats. The flight style falls on a midpoint between Arctic and Forster's Terns: slightly slower wingbeat than Arctic that appears choppy when compared to the matchless grace of Arctic Tern's flight, but faster and slightly smoother than the wingbeats of Forster's Tern. Often seen migrating diurnally, usually in loose flocks of 10–30+, sometimes at moderate heights above the water, but often skimming just above the waves.

**CALL** Frequent call a long, harsh, grating *Kee-yaaa*, usually with a slight hesitation between syllables. The second syllable tends to be drawn out, and then fades as though the tern has run out of breath. A sharp, frequently repeated *kip* serves as the common alarm call.

**RANGE** Breeds along the East Coast from South Carolina north through Atlantic Canada, across southern Canada west to western Alberta, in the Great Lakes region, and in the prairie potholes region of the Dakotas and Montana, and in a few scattered locations along the Gulf Coast. In coastal regions, small numbers tend to linger long after the bulk of Common Terns have already departed in fall, lingering latest along the Gulf Coast, where it is not unusual for small numbers to be present into December, though complete overwintering along the western Gulf Coast is rare. Confusion with Forster's Tern results in reports of far more overwintering birds than actually exist. After mid-December, assume all *Sterna* to be Forster's unless absolutely proven otherwise, even along the Gulf Coast. **World:** Widespread. All continents except Antarctica.

**SPECIES INFO** Found both coastally and across the interior, and often lives up to its name as the most abundant tern in many of the places where it is found, though it is rare or uncommon in much of the Interior West and along the Pacific coast. Along the Pacific coast, often more easily found during migration in offshore waters than along the immediate coast. Three subspecies: *S. h. hirundo*, *S. h. longipennis*, and *S. h. tibetana*. In North America, virtually all Common Terns are of the nominate subspecies, *S. h. hirundo*, though *S. h. longipennis* is a rare but regular stray to western Alaska, and there are a few records of individuals thought to be of *S. h. longipennis* from eastern North America.

**PLUMAGE INFO** All plumages are seen frequently in North America. Many migrants arrive in the early spring in nonbreeding plumage and molt into breeding plumage along the Gulf Coast before heading north. Likewise, in fall, many begin their body molt during migration, such that fall flocks of adults contain a mix of birds in full breeding plumage and mostly nonbreeding plumage (except for flight feathers), with many intermediates. Immature birds, which display significant plumage variation, are frequently found in the vicinity of breeding colonies, particularly in coastal locations, and in migration staging areas. The prevailing supposition is that immature birds that largely look like nonbreeding adults are "first-summer" birds, while those that have an appearance closer to that of breeding plumage adults but show white flecking on the cap and white patches amid the gray breast are "second-summer" birds. While this may be the typical pattern, studies of known-age birds suggest that the reality is far more complex. Instead, using the less definitive terms "first-summer type" and "second-summer type" provides for more accuracy, if less precision. Juveniles are regularly seen on the breeding grounds, but by fall, some have replaced mantle feathers, while others retain full juvenile plumage, but with so much fading that they resemble nonbreeding adults.

COMMON TERN 9 Breeding (alt.) adult. April, TX. In spring, the dark wedge in the outer half of the hand is far less apparent on most individuals than in midsummer. However, even when the wedge is not obvious, the oldest primary (from the prior fall) is side by side with the newest (replaced in early spring), and this slight contrast can be detected, although sometimes only in photos. By midsummer, most Common Terns show a very distinct dark wedge, but a handful look exactly like this and can be confused with Arctic Tern, as many observers are overly focused on the presence of a strongly contrasting dark wedge as the defining Common Tern trait. The bill is longer with a more extensive black tip than would be shown by an Arctic, but not as thick as that of Forster's, and the base is reddish rather than orange.

**COMMON TERN 10** Breeding (alt.) adult. Aug., MA. This individual is one of a small minority that replaced seven inner primaries in the spring, dramatically changing the shape of the dark wedge and recalling the pattern of Roseate Tern. Awareness that such variation exists is usually enough to avoid misidentification, as most birds with a reduced dark wedge display no other Roseate Tern traits.

**COMMON TERN 11** Molting (alt. > basic) adults and immature (first-cycle). Sept., GA. Variability is the name of the game with fall birds. While all show an obvious dark wedge, the degree to which the wedge contrasts with the rest of the wing varies individually quite a bit. Note that all these birds are similar in size and structure, and rather that get bogged down in the variability of the plumage, focus instead on the similarities in size, structure, and flight action across members of this flock to simplify identification.

COMMON TERN 12 Breeding (alt.) adult. April, TX. While Arctic Tern tends to show a narrow, sharply defined white cheek, most Common Terns have a white cheek that contrasts subtly with the pale gray neck and breast. It is the only member of the *Sterna* group that has tail-streamers that do not extend beyond the tips of the folded primaries during the breeding season, although broken streamers are common in all species.

COMMON TERN 13 Immature (second-summer type). Sept., GA. Immatures in summer with nearly complete caps but with pale foreheads are traditionally considered Common Terns in their second summer. However, recent studies have found that some Common Terns that are only one year old look identical, and other Common Terns that are more than two years old can also appear very similar. So, the moniker "second summer" often used in traditional field guides should be modified to "second-summer type" to acknowledge this uncertainty, while still conveying, to those familiar with the traditional term, a clear idea of what a bird described this way should look like. The term "immature" could also be used, as it is an accurate term, but is also broad and the only picture it paints is "not adult." The dark secondary bar is an underrated identification trait for Common Tern. It is most noticeable on immature birds, but many adults also show a narrow secondary bar. Forster's Tern very rarely shows a smudgy, indistinct secondary bar, but any well-defined secondary bar is diagnostic of Common Tern.

COMMON TERN 14 Juvenile and breeding (alt.) adult. Aug., MA. Sand Lance are an important food source for Common Tern, and breeding success is often linked to the availability of this fish. On this juvenile, nearly all the black on the head is behind the eye, and the eye appears isolated on the face, as opposed to the black on the head of juvenile Arctic Tern, which wraps around the eye; the eye is lost amid the black plumage.

COMMON TERN 15 Juveniles. Aug., MA. Juvenile Common Terns show significant variation in coloration. The dark carpal bars of both birds are largely hidden in this posture, though hints of it can be seen underneath the scapulars. The paler bird is very similar to a juvenile Arctic Tern, but note the bright white eyelid and longer legs.

**COMMON TERN 16** Juvenile comparison: fresh (left) and faded (right). July, NJ/Aug., MA. The soft buff color on the head and back of fresh juveniles fades quickly. The leading and trailing edges of the wing show a grayer area that sets off the paler area in the middle of the wing, whereas on juvenile Arctic Tern, the palest area of the wing is the white secondaries.

**COMMON TERN 17** Juvenile with juvenile Forster's Tern. Aug., NJ. Kevin T. Karlson. The head pattern of the juveniles of these species is distinctive, as is the peach-colored wash to the back of the Forster's Tern. The dark shoulder bar on the Common Tern is an obvious difference that is often cited. A far less known trait is the dark tertial centers of the Forster's Tern, unique among juvenile *Sterna*. The smaller head and bill and shorter legs of the Common Tern are useful traits at all ages.

**COMMON TERN 18** Nonbreeding (basic) adults with Forster's and Royal Terns and Herring and Laughing Gulls. Oct., NJ. A *Sterna* tern with entirely black primaries is usually, but not always, a Common Tern. At some points in the year, some Forster's Terns may also show black primaries. Note the primary color of the immature Forster's Tern in the background. During the spring and early summer, the only Common Terns that show entirely black primaries are immature birds, but by fall, many adults show this as well. Notice also the white lower eyelid on the right-hand Common Tern, and while there is faint mottling that extends below the eye, it does not connect. In Arctic Tern, the eyelid is dark, and there is a narrow black band underneath the eyelid.

**COMMON TERN 19** First-cycle and molting (basic > alt.) adults with Willet. April, TX. The two adults in the background highlight the variation that can be seen in the spring, when birds arrive along the Gulf Coast and immediately initiate the molt into breeding plumage. Notice how the dark carpal bar extends forward and wraps around under the wing on the first bird, a pattern seen only on immature Common Terns.

COMMON TERN 20 Juvenile. Sept., NJ. By September, many have begun to acquire smooth gray backs like those of adults. This individual has not done so, having maintained juvenile plumage, although the characteristic brown and buff highlights of fresh juvenile plumage have been lost. Juveniles show some orange at the base of the bill in fall, although some have just a hint (as here), while others show nearly as much as fresh juveniles. In contrast, the bills of juvenile Arctic Terns become completely black much faster, and by fall, most are entirely black-billed.

COMMON TERN 21 Molting (alt. > basic) adults and first-cycle with Bonaparte's Gull. Sept., OH. Adults begin a molt to nonbreeding plumage during fall migration, so individuals within most flocks in fall exhibit a wide variety of appearances ranging from nearly full breeding to nearly full nonbreeding plumage (although without new flight feathers), as well as various stages of transition.

**COMMON TERN 22** Immature (first-summer type). May, FL. Many immature birds in spring and summer look very similar to adults in fall entering nonbreeding plumage. It would be highly unusual for an immature Forster's Tern to have entirely dark primaries in May (though some have blackish outer primaries) and extremely rare for an immature Arctic to show entirely blackish primaries in spring, so that feature alone is a very strong indication that the bird in question is a Common Tern. The obvious shoulder bar, the head pattern, and the leg and bill lengths all confirm it as a Common Tern.

**COMMON TERN 23** Breeding (alt.) adult Siberian Common Tern (*S. h. longipennis*). June, AK. The Siberian subspecies of Common Tern is a scarce visitor to western Alaska, and individuals that show characteristics of this subspecies have been observed very rarely on the Atlantic coast of North America and in western Europe. Individuals have entirely dark bills in breeding plumage and are darker gray overall than nominate Common Tern, particularly on the breast.

**COMMON TERN 24** Breeding (alt.) adult Siberian Common Tern (*S. h. longipennis*). June, AK. In addition to the all-black bill and darker gray body, notice how the pale vanes on the inner webs of the outer primaries break up the dark trailing edge, making the black inner webs look like dark hash marks running down the wing. Nominate Common Terns have a more cohesive and blended dark trailing edge to the primaries, and the hash-marked appearance to the trailing edge seems a consistent feature of *S. h. longipennis*, though additional research would be useful to explore the variability of this trait.

**COMMON TERN 25** Breeding (alt.) Common Tern, probable *S. h. longipennis*. Sept., FL. John Groskopf. This individual has all the characteristics of a Siberian Common Tern. While nominate Common Tern shows significant variation in the fall, this individual lies outside that variation. The tone of the gray of both the upperparts and the underparts is a perfect match for a Siberian Common Tern. The leg color, nearly jet black, is spot on for Siberian Common Tern as well. Adult nominate Common Terns often show black bills in fall, but completely dark bare parts while retaining full alternate plumage is very unexpected. Combining that with the dark shade of the gray, if Siberian Common Tern can be identified out of range, this is it. This area is a major staging area for nominate Common Terns, and this individual may have joined a migrating flock of nominate Common Terns.

**ARCTIC TERN 1** Breeding (alt.) adult. June, AK. The stubby legs, short bill lacking a dark tip, and very rounded head all ensure that full breeding individuals are distinctive. Note also the perfectly uniform primaries, with no break in color or wear along the entire length. The tail-streamers are almost as long as those of Roseate Tern, projecting beyond the folded primaries.

## ARCTIC TERN *Sterna paradisaea*

L 11.8–13 in. (tail-streamers +2);
WS 30–33 in.; WT 3–4 oz.

**SIZE AND STRUCTURE** Nearly the same size as Common Tern but in direct comparison appears marginally smaller, slightly shorter-bodied and stockier. Almost neckless with a small, rounded head, a (typically) short bill, and distinctly short legs. During the summer, the tail is nearly as long as that of Roseate Tern, projecting well beyond the folded primaries when at rest. In flight, appears slightly front-heavy, with the wings set far forward on the body, though in breeding adults this appearance is balanced by the long tail. The wings are slimmer than those of Common Tern, particularly the hand, and are more swept back, appearing more strongly curved at a distance.

**BEHAVIOR** While Arctic Tern may forage using low-altitude dives at an oblique angle, like Common Tern, it also forages like Black Tern by swooping and plucking food from the surface without diving, the only *Sterna* that regularly displays this behavior. It also uses a terraced dive, dropping a short distance, then hovering, then another short drop and hover, before finally diving into the water. At sea, Arctic Terns may also employ vertical dives from greater heights. On the ground, short legs give an odd, stiff-legged, waddling gait that is quite distinct from the easier step of the longer-legged Common Tern. Arctic Tern is so aggressive in defending nesting areas that in Arctic regions, waterfowl and shorebirds often clump their nests around Arctic Tern colonies as protection against Arctic Foxes.

**FLIGHT** Buoyant, quick, and agile, with snappy wingbeats. Body typically bobs up and down gently with every wingbeat, more so than other *Sterna*, but it appears so smooth and natural that this motion is easily overlooked. Appears to almost float through the air when patrolling over nesting areas. Moves faster and more purposefully when foraging, and has an aggressive, powerful appearance when migrating through strong winds, with deeper wingbeats than those of Common Tern. In the breeding season, the long tail-streamers of adults bounce and flutter with every wingbeat, like Roseate Tern, but unlike Common and Forster's Terns.

ARCTIC TERN 2 Breeding (alt.) adult. June, AK. The short bill, small, rounded head, and neckless appearance combined with the heavy chest create a strongly front-heavy appearance balanced only by the long tail. The bill on this individual is longer than the average for Arctic Tern, a reminder that it is necessary to use multiple identification traits. These elements of structure are all subtle when taken individually, but when combined create a bird that is distinct from all other *Sterna* terns.

**ARCTIC TERN 3** Breeding (alt.) adult. June, AK. The cap extends farther down the face than Common Tern, extending below the eye. Arctic Tern has a darker gray body than that of Common Tern, the gray extending farther up the neck, so the white cheek is narrower than that of Common Tern. The intensity and extent of the gray on the body is much more evident in shadow or soft light, but can be completely washed out in bright sunlight or by light reflecting off water. In strong shadow, Common Terns can appear to nearly match the extent of gray shown by Arctic Terns, so use care when applying these traits, which are more useful in direct comparison rather than when attempting to apply them individually. The white line between the gape and black cap is also much narrower than that of Common Tern, and this trait can be easier to judge than the width of the white cheek.

**ARCTIC TERN 4** Breeding (alt.) adult (right) with Common Tern (left). July, MA. Ken Behrens. The striking differences in head shape and the uniform upper wing of the Arctic are particularly noticeably in this image. Note that on the Arctic Tern the head joins the body at almost the exact same point the wings jut out from it, so that it appears to lack a neck. Common Tern appears longer-necked and longer-billed. While it is easy to assess "neck length" on a photo, it is far more difficult in the field; neck length, though, has a strong effect on how you perceive the overall shape of the bird, even when the observation is brief. While the longer tail-streamers of the Arctic are visible, this image illustrates how easily the streamers fade into a pale background and should be considered a secondary trait in most situations. The completely uniform hand, lacking even a hint of the dark wedge shown by the Common Tern, is evident here.

**ARCTIC TERN 5** Juvenile. July, NS. Alix d'Entremont. Juvenile Arctic Terns, on average, show far less brown on the back than any other juvenile *Sterna*. What brownish tones they do have fade quickly, and their overall plumage tone is colder than other juvenile *Sterna*. The black on the head is extensive, giving them a unique hooded appearance with a dusky wash underneath the eye. The structure is typical of all Arctic Terns: notice, particularly, the short bill and legs and the small, golf ball–shaped head.

**ARCTIC TERN 6** Immature (first-summer type). July, MA. The uniform primaries with faint dark smudging along the leading edge of the wing are typical of immature Arctic Tern. The stocky, neckless body, rounded head, and short bill are also evident.

**ARCTIC TERN 7** Breeding (alt.) adult. June, AK. The deepest point of the body is far forward, enhancing a front-heavy appearance. The hand is thinner than that of Common Tern, and slightly more curved, giving the entire wing a more attenuated and aggressive shape than the wing of Common Tern.

**ARCTIC TERN 8** Breeding (alt.) adults. June, AK. Appear low-slung, with a very drawn out rear-end at a distance, with the tail-streamers projecting beyond the wingtips. The high-crowned, rounded heads and short bills further distinguish them from Common Terns. Arctic Tern is the darkest gray *Sterna* during the breeding season—its matte gray plumage seems to absorb the light that touches it, as opposed to Roseate Tern, which seems to reflect all the light that touches it.

ARCTIC TERN 9 Immature (first-summer type) with immature (second-summer type) Common Tern. July, MA. Ken Behrens. Notice the difference in head and bill shapes. First-cycle Arctic Terns vary from having a broad, smudgy, dark leading edge to the inner wing, like this individual, to having a very faint, diffuse, dark leading edge. In comparison, the leading edge on first-cycle Common Terns is narrower, but darker and more clearly defined, and they also have a dark secondary bar that this Arctic Tern clearly lacks. The white flecking across the belly of the Common Tern indicates that it is not a full adult, but, given the complete black cap, it is probably a second-summer or older immature.

ARCTIC TERN 10 Breeding (alt.) adult. June, AK. The thin, sharply defined, dark trailing edge to the primaries, the narrow white cheek, and the completely red bill are the classic adult traits; however, in the field, the easy buoyancy of Arctic Tern's elegant flight is the true distinguishing characteristic. Their bodies gently bounce with every wingbeat, but do so smoothly, so it appears utterly natural.

**ARCTIC TERN 11** Breeding (alt.) Arctic (left) and Common (right) Terns. July, MA. Left image by Ken Behrens. The primaries are all the same age on the Arctic, resulting in a uniform wing compared to the contrasting dark wedge of older outer primaries on the Common. The long tail of the Arctic is less rigid than that of the Common and bounces noticeably with the wingbeats. The hand is slightly narrower and more attenuated on the Arctic. Also note the broader, more clearly contrasting white trailing edge to the secondaries on the Arctic.

**ARCTIC TERN 12** Juveniles. July, NS. Alix d'Entremont. The legs are so short that their bellies almost brush the ground. Other *Sterna* terns can appear very similar if they are standing in a depression, so use this trait with care if you cannot see the entire leg. The short bills and rounded heads are distinctive. Notice how the back markings vary individually, but all have a cold gray appearance. They tend to have less orange at the base of the bill than other juvenile *Sterna*, and the bill turns mostly or entirely black by fall migration.

ARCTIC TERN 13 Immature (second-summer type). July, MA. Ken Behrens. The white spotting on the belly and flecking on the forehead, the darker bill, and the shorter tail are all indications of immaturity. The characteristic head and bill shapes are visible from every angle. The dark trailing edge to the primaries is sharply defined and very narrow. The angle of the wings in this photo limits the visibility of the translucent primaries, though hints of this translucency are still evident.

ARCTIC TERN 14 Immature (first-summer type). July, MA. Ken Behrens. The translucent vanes in the outer wing absolutely scream Arctic Tern, though whether they are visible depends on the angle of the light, and they are always more apparent in photos than in the field. Arctic Terns that lack tail-streamers appear extremely short-tailed, magnifying the front-weighted appearance of the body.

**RANGE** As the name suggests, it is primarily a high-latitude breeder, breeding in northern Canada from the Hudson Bay north, throughout Alaska, and along the Atlantic coast through the Atlantic Provinces south to Massachusetts. Along the Pacific coast, it breeds in northwestern British Columbia; south of described range, it breeds rarely and sporadically in small numbers, with the southernmost in the northern Puget Sound. **World:** Widespread, but primarily coastal/pelagic and difficult to observe away from the breeding grounds.

**CALL** Typical flight call a *Keee-ya*, like that of Common Tern, but higher in pitch and shorter in duration; the second syllable in particular is abbreviated, lacking the drawn-out, grating quality of Common Tern. Also a frequently given, sharp, quick *Kip* that is most often doubled, but can be given singly or in an extended series.

**SPECIES INFO** Arctic Tern is a pelagic migrant, well known for its migration from pole to pole, traveling from the Northern Hemisphere summer to the Southern Hemisphere summer, and in doing so, seeing more daylight than any other creature on earth. It is rarely seen from shore as a migrant, though it is occasionally encountered on pelagic trips off the East Coast, more regularly found offshore from the West Coast, and rarely from coastal promontories. While Arctic Tern is very rarely encountered inland, interior records are extremely widespread, suggesting that it can occur just about anywhere, and that small numbers may actually be regularly moving through the interior at high altitude. There are no described subspecies.

**PLUMAGE INFO** Full adult nonbreeding plumage is unknown in North America. Immature birds are often seen on the breeding grounds during the summer, rarely associating with Common Tern colonies just south of the breeding grounds of Arctic Tern. Juvenile plumage is seen on the breeding grounds, and they begin migration in full juvenile plumage, and so migrants in worn juvenile plumage can be encountered, particularly along the West Coast.

ARCTIC TERN 15 Immature (first-summer type). July, MA. Ken Behrens. The black-hooded appearance is superficially similar to that of first-summer type Common Tern, but once you key into the differences—black extending forward to cover the back of the crown and wrapping underneath the eye—it becomes distinctive. Also notice the rays of translucency in the primaries and translucent secondaries.

ARCTIC TERN 16 Juvenile. July, NS. Alix d'Entremont. Notice that the palest area of the wing is the white secondaries. More than any other plumage trait, this catches our eye with juveniles in flight. The overall paleness of the plumage contrasts with the large black hood, more extensive than that of any other juvenile *Sterna*.

ARCTIC TERN 17 Breeding (alt.) adults. June, MA. Ian Davies. Like most terns, the primaries of Arctic Tern become darker as they wear. This individual shows darker primaries than most adult Arctic Terns, particularly in the spring, but unlike Common Tern, all the primaries are evenly dark because they are all replaced at roughly the same time, lacking the molt limit in the middle primaries seen in Common Tern.

**ARCTIC TERN 18** Breeding (alt.) adults with a Short-billed Gull. May, AK. Robin Corcoran/USFWS. Arctic Terns usually migrate in pelagic waters far from shore. Flocks of migrants are rarely observed in most of North America, though during long periods of onshore winds that coincide with Arctic Tern migration, they can sometimes be seen from shore.

**ARCTIC TERN 19** Breeding (alt.) adult with Bonaparte's Gulls. July, NB. While most are noticeably short-billed, some, like this individual, have fairly sizable bills and may not conform to the idea of "classic" Arctic Tern. There are, however, few absolute field marks for terns, so it is useful to evaluate multiple features and to not rely too heavily on any single trait. Here we can see the uniform primaries, the entirely dark red bill, and the cap that extends below the eye, all traits of Arctic Tern.

## ROSEATE TERN *Sterna dougallii*

L 12–13 in. (tail-streamers +2);
WS 26–28 in.; WT 3.3–4.5 oz.

---

**SIZE AND STRUCTURE** Although very similar in size to Common Tern, often appears slightly to significantly smaller due to slim build, particularly in flight. Strikingly lean when compared to other *Sterna*, with longest tail of the group in breeding plumage, projecting well beyond folded wingtips. Bill long and spike-like, marginally longer than that of Common Tern, with slightly longer legs as well. In flight, the wings are slimmer, shorter, and held straighter in comparison to other *Sterna*, while the long tail ripples and bobs with every wingbeat. The body is subtly cone-shaped, deepest across the upper chest but with little or no noticeable chest expansion. Instead, the body tapers slightly, and this, coupled with the long bill and neck, creates a somewhat front-heavy appearance, particularly if the tail-streamers have broken off.

**BEHAVIOR** Tends to fly higher and patrols over a larger portion of water when foraging than other *Sterna*. In addition to hunting from greater heights, Roseate Tern also has distinctive foraging behavior in which it often beats its wings several times as it descends, accelerating into a dive in a Northern Gannet-like fashion. Consequently, Roseate Tern dives deeper, sometimes staying submerged for up to two seconds, whereas other *Sterna* make less adventurous dives, barely allowing the water to close over them before bursting back into the air.

**FLIGHT** The wingbeats are uniquely stiff and shallow, faster than Common Tern, powering a rapid, direct flight. Roseate Tern hovers less frequently than other *Sterna*, and when it does, it is with a frantic quality that recalls Least Tern. Flies quite high when foraging, 10–20 feet higher than other *Sterna*.

**CALL** Abrupt, harsh *CHI-rik*, strongly disyllabic, somewhat recalling the calls of Sandwich Tern, but not as rolling. Also a sharp *Kik* and a low, throaty *rrrraaa* alarm call. Juvenile calls are higher-pitched and more musical than those of adults.

ROSEATE TERN 1 Breeding (alt.) adult. June, NS. Alix d'Entremont. At first glance, this is a standard *Sterna* (although extremely pale), but the species has several distinctive traits. The bill remains entirely black for the spring and early summer. The bill color of this individual, taken June 9, is typical for early June, with the reddish base only beginning to appear. An extensive, readily apparent reddish base does not appear until late June or early July in most. Their tail-streamers are longer even than those of Arctic Tern, projecting far beyond the folded primaries, but are quite fragile and often break as a result.

ROSEATE TERN 2 Breeding (alt.) adult. Aug., MA. The species name refers to a soft pink flush shown by most adults in summer. It varies greatly in intensity between individuals but is diagnostic among *Sterna* terns if present. The color is so subtle that photos rarely depict it accurately, and it is more clearly seen in the field. The folded primaries show a complete white trailing edge—a particularly useful trait of Roseate Tern as it is present in all plumages. When they do have an extensively red-based bill, the red extends out farther on the upper mandible than on the lower mandible, so the division of black and red has the appearance of the letter Z turned on its side.

ROSEATE TERN 3 Breeding (alt.) adult. May, MA. Ian Davies. Lithe, long-tailed, long-billed, and narrow-winged, the structure of Roseate Tern is the most distinct outlier among the *Sterna* terns, recalling a small Sandwich Tern. Throughout the spring, until the end of May, their glossy, entirely black bills serve as an immediate means of distinguishing Roseate Terns from other *Sterna* terns.

ROSEATE TERN 4 Adult, two immatures, and three Common Terns (front left, background, and far background). Aug., MA. Roseate Tern is strikingly pale, almost seeming to glow compared to Common Terns, and this impression of overwhelming paleness is often the first clue to pick out a distant Roseate; the pink blush is usually visible only at close range. The bold white inner webs of the primaries are clearly displayed on the spread wing (particularly visible on the right wing of this bird), while the black in the wing is mostly on the outer webs and around the feather shafts of the outer 2–3 primaries in most breeding adults. The broad white inner webs create a thin white trailing edge on the folded primaries (visible on the leftmost Roseate), a definitive trait present on all Roseate Terns.

**RANGE** Two distinct breeding populations in North America: one in the Caribbean (including a handful in the Florida Keys) and a northeastern population from Long Island to Nova Scotia. This pattern of widely divided breeding locations is reflected in the Old World, where the species has multiple breeding populations in both tropical and temperate habitats, often separated by thousands of miles. Small numbers, particularly nonbreeding immature individuals, are found south of the breeding grounds in the Mid-Atlantic region during the summer, usually in the company of Common Terns. A large percentage of the northeastern breeding population makes its way to staging areas near Cape Cod, then departs en masse within just a few days in mid-September. **World:** Widespread, but very spottily distributed, in Europe, Africa, Asia, Australia, the Caribbean, Central America, and northern South America.

**SPECIES INFO** Primarily pelagic in both spring and fall, and so migratory movements are rarely observed, as the species completely vacates North America after the breeding season. Though the complete picture of the wintering grounds of this species is still emerging, it seems that the majority of the North American breeders spend the nonbreeding season off the northeastern coast of South America. Roseate Terns have been extensively studied and, due to that attention, a huge percentage of the North American breeders are banded. Should you see a banded leg while scanning a flock of *Sterna* terns, always check to see if it is attached to a Roseate Tern. There are five described subspecies, though they are weakly differentiated; only the nominate, *S. d. dougallii*, occurs in North America.

**PLUMAGE INFO** Adults in nonbreeding plumage are very unlikely to be encountered, because adults depart North America while still in breeding plumage. Breeding adults are the most likely Roseate Terns observers will encounter, though immature birds are also regularly seen on the breeding grounds and, occasionally, with large gatherings of Common Tern south of the breeding range. Juveniles are regularly seen on the breeding grounds from midsummer through the departure of the species in early fall.

**ROSEATE TERN 5** Breeding (alt.) adult (far left) with one adult and two juvenile Common Terns. Aug., MA. Cloudy conditions, as in this image, make the paler color of Roseate Tern compared to Common and Arctic Terns even more apparent. Bright sun washes out the grayer color of Common and Arctic Terns, blunting the difference in color between these species and Roseate Tern. On a cloudy day, though, notice how the color of this adult Roseate absolutely pops compared to the adult Common Tern standing next to it. The flatter crown and slimmer, more pointed bill of the Roseate are also obvious here.

**ROSEATE TERN 6** Breeding (alt.) adult. Aug., MA. The ultra-slender body, showing almost no expansion at the chest, is typical of Roseate Tern. The lengthy tail-streamers of all the *Sterna* species are very delicate and prone to break, creating a more abbreviated appearance. Because of their long bills and necks, Roseate Terns tend to have a front-heavy appearance in flight, particularly noticeable on short-tailed individuals, while birds with full-length tails appear more balanced. During the breeding season, the feet are usually much brighter than the bills, a trait that other adult breeding *Sternas* rarely show. Roseate Tern also lacks a distinct dark trailing edge to the undersides of the primaries, unlike Common and Arctic Terns.

**ROSEATE TERN 7** Immature (first-summer type) with a Sandwich Tern. April, FL. Mike Ostrowski. Roseate Tern is an outlier among *Sterna* terns with some traits that recall a Sandwich Tern in miniature. The bill and body structure of Roseate Tern, as well as the overall coloration, are very much like Sandwich Tern. Many of the plumage traits of this first-summer type bird, however, are more comparable to an immature Common Tern. The pattern of the dark hood is quite similar to that of an immature Common Tern. It also shows a dark shoulder bar, though it is weaker than that of a comparably aged Common Tern, and a dark wedge developing in the middle primaries like a Common Tern. However, this bird's pale gray color, entirely white tail, and extensive white tips to the feathers on the trailing edge of the wing leave no doubt that it is an immature Roseate.

**ROSEATE TERN 8** Breeding (alt.) adult. Aug., MA. Roseates are strikingly slender, far more so than other *Sterna*, almost to the point of appearing emaciated or, with their long bills and tails, as if they have been stretched lengthwise. The red base of the bill is fading on this late summer adult. This individual has three dark outer primaries (normally two), so while most Roseate Terns in flight show only a narrow band of black along the leading edge of the primaries, this individual would show a narrow dark wedge, thus its wing pattern would be more similar to that of a Common Tern. The leg color of adult Roseates during the summer is an intense raspberry red-orange, unique among North American *Sterna*. Unlike the bill color, the leg color does not fade before they undertake fall migration.

**ROSEATE TERN 9** Breeding (alt.) adult. June, NS. Alix d'Entremont. The long, spike-like bill remains almost entirely black for most of June in adults, a very eye-catching trait. Unlike in Common and Arctic Terns, in Roseate Terns the underside of the wing lacks a dark trailing edge to the primaries. Roseate Terns dive from greater heights and stay under the water longer than other *Sterna*.

**ROSEATE TERN 10** Juvenile. Aug., MA. The finely streaked forecrown with a darker line through the eyes to the nape is typical of juvenile Roseate Tern. From a distance, these features give the head a dirty appearance, unique among first-cycle *Sterna* terns. The dark scallops on the back are also unique, although this individual has already replaced a few back feathers. The well-defined, blackish subterminal V markings on the tertials are more defined than the brownish, weak subterminal U marking on the tertials of juvenile Common and Arctic Terns. The white trailing edge of the folded primaries is present in all plumages.

**ROSEATE TERN 11** Juvenile (front) with juvenile Common Tern, and adult *Sterna* in the background. Aug., MA. The fine streaking on the forehead and crown of a juvenile Roseate Tern gives it a dirty-headed appearance—compare to the juvenile Common Tern behind it. Other juvenile *Sterna* have dull orange bases to the bills (though those of juvenile Arctic Tern quickly turn black), whereas juvenile Roseate Terns have black bills. The bold shoulder bar on this juvenile Common Tern that wraps under the shoulder exceeds the strongest shoulder bar of any Roseate or Arctic Tern. *What is the adult tern in the background?*

**ROSEATE TERN 12** Juvenile. July, NS. Alix d'Entremont. Note how even the outer primaries have noticeable white tips, a trait no other juvenile *Sterna* possesses to a noticeable degree. It has a dark secondary bar and dark shoulder bar, like a juvenile Common Tern, but both features are extremely washed out compared to those of juvenile Common Tern. While adult Roseate Terns have entirely white tails, juveniles often show gray outer webs to their tail feathers like those of a Common Tern. This bird is so recently fledged that the bill and outer primaries are not fully grown, changing the structure somewhat. Juvenile Roseates fledge more quickly, and fly more strongly, than juvenile Common Terns.

**ROSEATE TERN 13** Quiz. Aug., MA. *Of the six closest terns, four are Roseate and two are Common. Which are which, and what are their ages?*

**ROSEATE TERN 14** Breeding (alt.) adult. Aug., MA. Roseate Terns tend to fly higher than other *Sterna* terns, and a combination of their high flight (forcing the viewer to look up at them), brilliant white plumage, and stiff wingbeats creates the impression of a miniature tropicbird. Note the lack of a dark trailing edge to the outer primaries, while Common and Arctic Terns show clear dark trailing edges.

**ROSEATE TERN 15** Breeding (alt.) adult (front left) with breeding (alt.) adult Common Tern. Aug., MA. The immediate impression is of an extremely pale and slender tern with slimmer wings than the Common Tern. Only the outer two primaries are dark, whereas the Common has a large dark wedge. Many Common Terns show a dark secondary bar, as this Common Tern does, while the other adult *Sterna* terns never show such a strong, complete dark secondary bar.

**ROSEATE TERN 16** Breeding (alt.) adults and immature. May, FL. Dan Irizarry. As they are primarily a pelagic migrant, Roseate Terns are rarely observed in active migration like this flock. As the two upper birds are starting a downward wingbeat, notice how the wings are nearly straight, not swept back like on other *Sterna*.

**ROSEATE TERN 17** Breeding (alt.) adult (center) and juvenile (left) with juvenile Common Tern. Aug., MA. Note the leaner bodies and flatter crowns of both Roseates compared to the slightly plumper, more round-headed Common Tern.

**ROSEATE TERN 18** Breeding (alt.) adult with Common Tern. Aug., MA. The differences between this classic example of a Common Tern and this typical Roseate Tern are glaring. Only the outer primaries are dark on the Roseate, as opposed to the extensive wedge of dark primaries on the Common. The back of the Roseate is so pale it almost blends with the white rump, whereas the rump contrasts distinctly with the back on the Common. Also compare the slender and more pointed bill shape of the Roseate Tern to the thicker-based bill of the Common Tern.

**ROSEATE TERN 19** Immatures with Common Terns. Aug., MA. Here, two immature Roseate Terns are sandwiched between three Common Terns. The bird on the right shows an extensive pale forehead, a trait associated with first-summer Roseate Terns, while the bird on the left has only a pale-flecked forehead, a trait associated with second-summer Roseate Terns. However, these are only tendencies, not solid criteria for aging these birds. The reality is that birds with multi-year maturation processes often do not conform to our ideas of what a bird of a certain age should look like. Embrace the very real uncertainty that exists, and use the terms "first-summer type" and "second-summer type," or just "immature."

## *STERNA* TERN IDENTIFICATION

Medium-sized terns, or *Sterna* terns, are the most consistently difficult terns to identify. Even so, most well-seen *Sterna* are readily identifiable, with some practice. There is a tendency in identification treatments of *Sterna* terns to focus on minutia and to fail to adequately highlight the differences between each species in size and structure. The following photo section will address some of the issues of *Sterna* identification, while attempting to not blow the difficulty out of proportion. As you never know what species will be encountered in the field, the photos are not in any particular order. Instead, by jumping from one subject to the next, we are following principles of mixed learning, which may seem scattershot, but actually cause information to be embedded in long-term memory more effectively than a more ordered approach.

*STERNA* TERN 1 *Sterna* terns. April, TX. Ken Behrens. Distant *Sterna* silhouettes are challenging to identify. There are some subtle wingbeat traits that might give them away. While on the Texas coast in April these birds are almost certainly Forster's or Common Terns, could you rule out a stray Arctic in the group with certainty? Sometimes it's better to stop the ID process at *Sterna* sp. The individual structures of these birds, the spacing between individuals, and the shape of the flock are all typical of *Sterna* terns in migratory groups, or with birds moving between roost and feeding locations.

Common Tern (Aug., FL)

Arctic Tern (June, AK)

Forster's Tern (April, TX)

Roseate Tern (Aug., MA)

***STERNA* TERN 2** Breeding (alt.) adult *Sterna* terns.

***STERNA* TERN 3** Juvenile *Sterna* terns.

Common Tern (July, NJ)

Arctic Tern (July, NS. Alix d'Entremont)

Forster's Tern (July, NJ)

Roseate Tern (Aug., MA)

***STERNA* TERN 4** Breeding (alt.) adult Common Terns and an immature Arctic Tern. May, NC. Jason Denesevich. Note the thinner, more tapered hand of the Arctic Tern in the lead. Also notice the uniform gray color of the hand, lacking the clear molt limit in the hand of the Common Tern next to it.

***STERNA* TERN 5** Breeding (alt.) adult Common and Roseate Terns. June, NY. Douglas Gochfeld. Even with a photo, your eye is probably drawn to the two glowing white Roseate Terns, and the effect is even stronger in the field. Roseate Terns retain their black bills all through spring and early summer and should not show large amounts of red on the bill until July.

**STERNA TERN 6** Breeding (alt.) adult Common and Arctic Terns with Ring-billed Gull. May, ON. Daniel Riley. The high crown, rounded head, and short bill of the Arctic Tern scream for recognition. Note how the belly of the Arctic is almost brushing the pipe it is standing on.

**STERNA TERN 7** Breeding (alt.) adult Common and Roseate Terns. June, MA. Ken Behrens. Direct comparison blows away the idea that *Sterna* terns are the same size and shape. Taking traits that are easily discernable in direct comparison and applying them when no comparison is available is a skill that takes time to learn. It begins with the direct comparison, which highlights the exact differences between two similar species. Drink in opportunities for comparisons—they are the most effective situations for durable learning.

***STERNA* TERN 8** Juvenile Common Tern and first-summer type Arctic Tern. July, NB. Ted D'Eon. Note the tiny feet and short legs of the Arctic Tern compared to those of the Common Tern. There is actually a very perceptible difference in the way the two species walk due to the different foot/leg length: Arctic Tern has a flat-footed, waddling gait, while Common Tern takes more natural steps. Immature Arctic Terns often show a dark carpal bar, but it is usually gray and muted. Also note that the primaries are of a single generation and there are black markings underneath the eye.

***STERNA* TERN 9** Molting (basic > alt.) adult Forster's Tern with molting adult Common Terns. April, TX. Common Terns arrive on the Gulf Coast primarily in nonbreeding plumage and molt into breeding plumage at the same time as Forster's Terns. Forster's acquire their black cap in a random pattern that results in this salt-and-pepper pattern, while Common Terns acquire the cap in a more orderly, back-to-front pattern, which can be seen on the two Common Terns behind the Forster's. The dark head markings of Common Tern often have a matte appearance tinged with brown, while those of Forster's are glossy black.

*STERNA* TERN 10 Breeding (alt.) adult Common and Arctic Terns. May, NJ. Jason Denesevich. In this perfect wing comparison note the long, thin, clearly defined dark trailing edge on the Arctic Tern, while the opposite wing shows the uniform gray hand, lacking the dark wedge of the Common Tern. Also note the slimmer hand of the Arctic Tern and the way the pale cheek contrasts sharply with the gray lower face.

*STERNA* TERN 11 Breeding (alt.) adult Common Terns. June, NY. Douglas Gochfeld. *Amid this group of Common Terns is one additional species of* Sterna *tern. Which bird is it, and what is the species?*

**STERNA TERN 12** Forster's Tern (second-cycle). May, TX. Forster's Terns, in their second fall, undergo a molt that includes only inner primaries. From midwinter through the second spring, this causes a pattern to develop that closely mimics that of Common Terns in summer. They often have short tail-streamers, increasing the similarity to Common Terns. Birders focused on the dark wedge as the primary identification trait for Common Tern can easily mistake second-cycle Forster's as Common Terns. To correctly identify these birds requires a good eye for the size and structural differences between Common and Forster's Terns combined with a greater focus on details than is typically required to identify these species. Note the outermost tail feather, which has a white outer web and gray inner web, a typical Forster's trait. Also note that the rump is whitish, contrasting slightly with the gray lower back and center of the tail. There is a broad white gap between the base of the bill and the cap. This individual has the typical orange bill base of a Forster's, but many of these second-cycle birds show a mostly dark bill, increasing the difficulty.

**STERNA TERN 13** Breeding (alt.) adult Common Tern. Aug., MA. The lower eyelid of Common Tern is white in all plumages, and the area immediately below the eyelid is also always white. Seemingly a small trait, it can actually be seen well in the field, and also shows well in photos. Arctic Terns have dark lower eyelids and typically a narrow, unbroken dark band running underneath the eyelid.

*STERNA* TERN 14 Mixed *Sterna* terns. July, MA. Ken Behrens. *Amid this group of Common Terns are at least nine Arctic Terns. Can you find them all?*

*STERNA* TERN 15 Breeding (alt.) adult Common x Roseate Tern hybrid. June, NB. Ted D'Eon. This bird was banded as a chick in a nest attended by an adult Roseate Tern. Noticing that the downy plumage of the chick was the wrong color for a Roseate Tern, the researchers banded it as a suspected hybrid. As an adult, it looks mostly like a Roseate Tern, but a Roseate should not show such an extensively red-based bill in early June (June 8). An additional point of evidence is that the bird molted only six inner primaries in the spring, in line with the pattern shown by Common Tern, not eight, as expected for Roseate. It has a pale gray breast, a reduced white trailing edge to the primaries, and a shorter tail than expected for a Roseate. All these traits could perhaps be overlooked, with the possible exception of the bill color, but together, they add up to a Common x Roseate hybrid. The call of this bird was not recorded but is a very key piece of the puzzle for any suspected *Sterna* hybrid. Such birds are thought to be fertile, and the idea of what the second-generation offspring would look like is alarming for ID purposes, regardless of whether it mated with a Common Tern or a Roseate Tern.

***STERNA* TERN 17** Breeding (alt.) adult Roseate Tern and breeding adult Common Tern. July, ME. Notice the slender, tube-like shape of the Roseate grading into those incredible tail-streamers. The bill of the Roseate in early July is only beginning to turn red. Notice how the Roseate lacks a dark trailing edge to the undersides of the primaries, while the Common Tern shows this trait clearly.

***STERNA* TERN 16** Probable Common x Arctic Tern hybrid. June, ME. The author identified this bird at a distance as an Arctic Tern by flight style and photographed it. The photos, however, clearly show a bird that is not an Arctic Tern. It has a distinct Common Tern–like molt limit in the middle primaries that creates a weak dark wedge in the outer primaries, eliminating Arctic Tern. The bill length and tail length are also more in line with Common Tern. It may in fact be a particularly dark Common Tern, but it has some traits that suggest it may actually be a rare Common x Arctic Tern hybrid. The black cap extends far enough down that there is a thin strip of black below the eye, the pale wedge between the base of the bill and the cap is very narrow, and the axillaries are gray. Additional traits that suggest Arctic Tern are the chest-heavy appearance, the very slender hand, the overall darkness of the gray plumage, the deep reddish color of the bill, the lack of black marking in the secondaries, the white trailing edge to the wing extending into the inner primaries, and the highly contrasting leading edge of the wing. The flight style of this individual was distinctly different from numerous other Common Terns in the vicinity and is what initially suggested Arctic Tern. At least one documented Common x Arctic Tern hybrid from a known mixed pair showed Common Tern–like molt limits. In general, hybrid *Sterna* are likely more regular than is currently recognized.

***STERNA* TERN 18** Breeding (alt.) adult Arctic Tern. Sept., OR. Roy W. Lowe. This bedraggled individual shows that some Arctic Terns can have the dark primaries more often associated with Common Terns in fall. Such a bird could be challenging, particularly if it occurred in an area where observers do not often see Arctic Terns. Note the bill color and shape, the short legs, and the narrow white wedge between the cap and the gape line.

# LITTLE TERNS: GENUS *STERNULA*

**The word *sternula* translates directly to "small tern." The genus includes seven species, found nearly worldwide, with only one, Least Tern, occurring in North America. The genus is quite homogenous; all species are quite similar to Least Tern, though as the name implies, Least Tern is (marginally) the smallest *Sternula* and the smallest tern in the world.**

## LEAST TERN *Sternula antillarum*

L 8–9 in.; WS 19–21 in.; WT 1–1.6 oz.

**SIZE AND STRUCTURE** The smallest North American tern, noticeably smaller than Black Tern. Tiny, to the point that little else matters from an identification standpoint, though a more critical look reveals a stocky body; a small, flat-crowned head; and a disproportionally large bill. In flight, the wings are long but strikingly slender, while the tail is short and disappears at all but close range, emphasizing the heavy-set body.

**BEHAVIOR** Gregarious, noisy, and highly energetic. When roosting, they gather shoulder to shoulder in tight pods of tens to hundreds, often on the fringes of flocks of other terns, looking like a misplaced group of nervous grade-school children at a high-school hangout. When disturbed, these pods explode into flight, with every bird uttering its shrill war cry at the top of its voice. In the vicinity of breeding colonies, positively pugnacious, attacking interlopers of all descriptions.

**FLIGHT** Extremely quick, stiff wingbeats, and unstable flight—jerking, bobbing, and frequently stopping to hover. Body bobs slightly with every wingbeat, adding to the impression of instability. Least Tern always seems to be in a hurry but not absolutely certain of where it is going, the exact opposite of the other small tern seen in North America, the Black Tern, which has a graceful, floating flight style.

LEAST TERN 1 Breeding (alt.) adult. May, FL. The only tern with a bright yellow bill and white forehead wedge in North America. Unlike some terns, Least Terns arrive in spring already in breeding plumage, and most depart the northern parts of their breeding range while still in this plumage. Additionally, the combination of their tiny size and pale bill color is unique within the North American range.

**LEAST TERN 2** Breeding (alt.) adult with Semipalmated Plover and Dunlin. April, FL. The smallest tern in North America, the size of a small shorebird. Note how all the weight falls in front of the legs, creating a chest-heavy appearance, balanced by the long slender wings that attenuate the impression of the body. Also note that they are absolutely tiny.

**LEAST TERN 3** Breeding (alt.) adults. April, TX. Like most terns, Least Terns perform complex displays involving ceremonial feeding, often followed by copulation. During these displays, they constantly emit a series of high-pitched screeches. The number of black outer primaries visible in the summer is 2–3 and varies far less than in some of the larger terns, such as Common. When perched, the dark outer primaries are barely noticeable.

**LEAST TERN 4** Breeding (alt.) adult with Common Tern. July, NJ. Medium-sized terns like this Common Tern (right) dwarf Least Tern. The head of the Least Tern is distinctly smaller and flatter-crowned than that of the Common, but note how the bill size approaches that of the Common. Because they are so strikingly tiny, other details of Least Tern structure are often ignored, but they do have a stocky chest, a disproportionally huge bill, a tiny head, and a short tail.

**LEAST TERN 5** Breeding (alt.) adult with chick. June, NJ. Kevin T. Karlson. They nest on beaches and sandbars, laying eggs directly into small scrapes in the sand. Their eggs and, once hatched, nestlings are camouflaged to blend into these habitats. Unfortunately, the same habitats are often areas prized by humans, bringing the birds in conflict with human recreation and expansion. Fortunately, most populations of Least Tern receive federal or state protections.

LEAST TERN 6 Breeding (alt.) adults. April, TX. The structure of Least Terns in flight is distinctive—proportionally large-bodied, with exceptionally narrow wings and tiny heads. Least Tern wingbeats are extremely rapid, often almost blurring, giving a hummingbird-like effect. Traveling flocks are nearly always single species; they do not mix readily with other terns in flight except briefly when leaving a mixed-species loafing area. Foraging usually occurs singly, a lone individual coursing back and forth parallel to the shoreline 8–15 feet above the water, at times gaining and losing altitude like a yo-yo, and making abrupt vertical dives.

LEAST TERN 7 Breeding (alt.) adults, molting (alt. > basic) adult, and immature (first-summer type). July, FL. In many areas, Least Terns migrate south before beginning to molt, but along the Gulf of Mexico and the southern Atlantic states, staging adult Least Terns often begin to molt their heads, like the birds on the far left and front right, before moving south. The bird directly behind the front right bird is likely an immature bird.

**LEAST TERN 8** Breeding (alt.) adults with Black Tern and Royal Tern. July, FL. The Royal Tern towers over this swarm of Least Terns. Even the dark-backed immature Black Tern is noticeably larger. Least Terns often gather in little clump-like flocks, on the edges of groups of other terns or in isolated single-species flocks. Least Terns in tightly packed knots of 30–50 on the fringes of flocks of larger birds are jarringly tiny and, therefore, distinctive.

**LEAST TERN 9** Immature (advanced first-summer type) with Black Tern. July, FL. In overall measurements, Least and Black Terns are fairly similar, but Black Tern has a much greater bulk and always appears noticeably larger. The darker color of Black Tern only adds to the appearance of greater bulk. The difference is even more evident in flight, where the broad wing of Black Tern and its easy, floating flight style are polar opposites from the narrow wings and manic flight style of Least Tern. The pale flecking on the crown and the large number of black outer primaries indicates this is likely not an adult.

**LEAST TERN 10** Breeding (alt.) adults. April, TX. Tight groups of Least Terns often explode off a beach nearly simultaneously when disturbed, flushed by a predator, or when going to do battle with a threat to their colony, real or perceived. They tend to stay in small, tightly packed clumps like this one, all members calling at the tops of their voices, giving the impression of a small, furious cloud.

**LEAST TERN 11** Juvenile, breeding (alt.) adult. July, FL. The dark, scalloped back is typical of juveniles. They usually begin molting these back feathers within a month of fledging, right before they depart the US. This individual has particularly dark scalloping; many juveniles have a less defined back pattern.

**RANGE** Breeds along the Gulf Coast, the East Coast north to Maine, southern California, and in the vicinity of major rivers and on some manmade reservoirs in the central U.S. north to North Dakota and eastern Montana. Winters primarily in pelagic waters off northern South America and in the southern Caribbean. Extremely rare anywhere in the U.S. during winter, with most records coming from the western Gulf Coast. **World:** Mexico, the Caribbean, Central America, and northern South America, more rarely farther south along both coasts of South America.

**CALL** Shrill, fast *KeeOW Kee-dik*, repeated frequently, as well as a *chit* given in a hurried series; also other shrill, angry utterances near nesting colonies. Oftentimes, numerous individuals are calling at once, and the sound washes over you as an indecipherable wall of shrill discord.

LEAST TERN 12 Immature (first-summer type) and breeding (alt.) adult. May, FL. The bird in the background is a first-summer type Least Tern. In general appearance, it shares some traits with first-summer type Common Terns, particularly since most North American birders associate Least Terns with yellow bills, but note the identical size and structure to the adult Least Tern in the foreground.

LEAST TERN 13 Immature (first-summer type). Aug., NJ. This immature bird looks much like a nonbreeding adult, but the shadow of the juvenile wing pattern, with whitish inner primaries and secondaries and a dark leading edge to the wing, indicates that it is an immature bird. Many of these birds stay on the nonbreeding grounds, but a few arrive in North America in spring, and more show up later in summer. Few birders encounter this plumage, so it can be confusing, but the tiny size trumps all other ID traits.

**LEAST TERN 14** First-summer comparison. Left image May, FL. Right image July, FL. These two birds are roughly the same age, indicating the broad variability that first-cycle birds can display. The bird on the left is similar to worn juvenile birds or nonbreeding adults, while the bird on the right is very similar to a breeding adult, except for the white-flecked crown, and could be confused with an adult molting out of breeding plumage. Note, however, that the folded primaries are almost entirely black on both, a typical trait of birds that are roughly a year old. Based on how birders typically interpret plumages in *Sterna* terns, it might be tempting to label the bird on the left "first-summer" and the one on the right "second-summer"; however, band returns of known-age birds inform us that first-cycle Least Terns are highly variable.

**LEAST TERN 15** Breeding (alt.) adult. May, NJ. Jesse Amesbury. The flight style of Least Tern has an impetuous quality, heightened by their tendency to make sudden, absolutely vertical dives. Adults typically show only two black outer primaries that form a narrow black band along the leading edge of the hand.

**SPECIES INFO** Three subspecies: Eastern Least Tern, *Sternula antillarum antillarum*, breeds on the East Coast and Gulf Coast; Interior Least Tern, *S. a. athalassos*, breeds on interior rivers; and California Least Tern, *S. a. browni*, breeds in southern California and the Baja Peninsula, but there are no consistent, field-discernable differences between these subspecies. Both California and Interior Least Terns are federally endangered, while Eastern Least Tern has state conservation status nearly everywhere, giving it the dubious distinction of being the North American tern with the most widespread conservation challenges.

**PLUMAGE INFO** The overwhelming majority are adults in breeding plumage. Complete nonbreeding plumage is essentially unknown in North America. The first-summer type plumage is seen occasionally in North America and has the appearance of a tiny first-summer Common Tern, which can be confusing to birders unaware of this plumage. Juvenile plumage can be seen in the vicinity of breeding colonies in late summer, but is rapidly lost. In early fall, shortly before migration, particularly along the Gulf Coast, adults begin to molt head plumage, and their bills begin darkening, rapidly attaining an appearance similar to immature birds during this period.

# MARSH TERNS: GENUS *CHLIDONIAS*

The word *chlidonias* is a reworking of the ancient Greek word for "swallow." Worldwide, there are four species in the genus *Chlidonias*, one of which occurs in North America regularly, and two of which are vagrants. While most terns are garbed in white, the *Chlidonias* terns feature much darker colorations, managing to meet or exceed the reputation terns have for beauty and elegance. They are species typically associated with freshwater lakes and marshes with abundant emerging vegetation, though in the winter, Black Tern is largely pelagic. These terns delicately dip rather than dive for their food, and have broad wings for their size, giving their flight a floating, hypnotic quality that is difficult to tear your eye from. As a group, they have a rounded wing shape, like a bent bow, that is distinctly less angular than that of most terns.

## BLACK TERN *Chlidonias niger*

L 9–9.7 in.; WS 23.5–25.5 in.; WT 2.1–3 oz.

**SIZE AND STRUCTURE** Slightly larger than Least Tern, and obviously smaller than Common Tern. Small, with a slightly pudgy, compact body; a delicate, rounded head; and a short, slightly forked tail that often appears squared off. The wings are disproportionally short, and quite broad through the hand, so that the wing has significant surface area. Starting at the wrist, the leading edge of the wing curves back modestly to the wingtip, whereas in most terns, the leading edge is a sharp, nearly straight line.

**BEHAVIOR** While some species of terns use surface dipping as an occasional method of feeding, Black Tern specializes in it. It swoops and plucks prey smoothly from the surface, causing barely a ripple.

BLACK TERN 1 Breeding (alt.) adult. May, ND. Breeding adults are unmistakable and stunning, a welcome sight every time they are encountered. The head is smoothly rounded, and the body gives a rounded, slightly plump impression. Unlike the nominate subspecies found in the Old World, the head and body are evenly black.

**BLACK TERN 2** Breeding (alt.) adult. July, FL. Glossy black adults are a rare treat along the Gulf Coast, usually seen as late spring or very early fall migrants; most adults are in body molt as they pass through the southern tier of states in both directions. A tiny bit of the reddish gape can be seen, but when the birds are calling on the breeding grounds, the red mouth provides the little bit of color needed to make the rest of their gray and black plumage pop.

**BLACK TERN 3** Breeding (alt.) adults. May, ND. Ken Behrens. Stunning! Their easy, floating flight style is as beautiful as their garb. The second bird from the front shows the classic profile, with the gently curved hand and bill tilted slightly downward. Note also the short-tailed appearance. Black Tern's wings are slightly broader, shorter, and not as tapered as those of most terns, creating a wing silhouette that is characteristic of marsh terns but differs from that of other terns.

**BLACK TERN 4** Molting (alt. > basic) adult with juvenile Least Terns. July, FL. Still unmistakable, but exhibiting the typical mottled appearance of Black Tern during both migrations in most locations. The rounded head, long neck, and dumpy body give a pigeon-like impression.

**BLACK TERN 5** Breeding (alt.) adult with Least Tern. July, FL. While Black Terns measure only marginally larger than Least Terns, they have significantly greater bulk, and the dark plumage heightens the impression of greater size.

**BLACK TERN 6** Immature (first-summer type). July, FL. Migrant flocks in midsummer and early fall often include a few first-summer type birds, which can be difficult to distinguish from molting adults. However, the old, dirty brown greater coverts on this individual indicate that it is not yet an adult. The precise progression of immature plumages has yet to be satisfactorily described for Black Tern, so aging in Black Tern is clouded by a particularly complex series of molts in the first cycle and tremendous individual variation. This individual has an older, more pointed, outermost primary (the protruding feather on each wing) and some very worn, brownish coverts, suggesting that it is about a year old. For birds that look similar but lack discernable retained juvenile plumage, the term "first-summer type" imparts both what the bird is likely to look like and the lack of certainty as to its exact age.

**BLACK TERN 7** Juvenile. Aug., NJ. Cameron Rutt. The rich brown fringes to the slate-colored back feathers combined with the oddly shaped dark cap ensure that juvenile Black Terns are both distinctive and beautiful, though in an understated way. Juvenile White-winged Tern is similar, but has paler wing coverts that contrast with a more solidly brown back, and lacks the dark patch extending forward from the shoulder shown by Black Tern.

**BLACK TERN 8** Adult and chicks. June, BC. Kevin T. Karlson. Black tern most often nests on floating mats of vegetation amid marshes near open patches of water where it can forage. The rich brown fledglings are as striking and distinctive as their parents.

**BLACK TERN 9** Juvenile. Aug., NC. The wings are quite broad, giving tremendous surface area to the wing for their size, facilitating a smooth, floating flight style. The gray wash down the flanks identifies this individual as belonging to the North American subspecies of Black Tern, *C. n. surinamensis*. The juveniles of the Old World subspecies, *C. n. niger*, have entirely white flanks, but a record has yet to be confirmed from the U.S. or Canada.

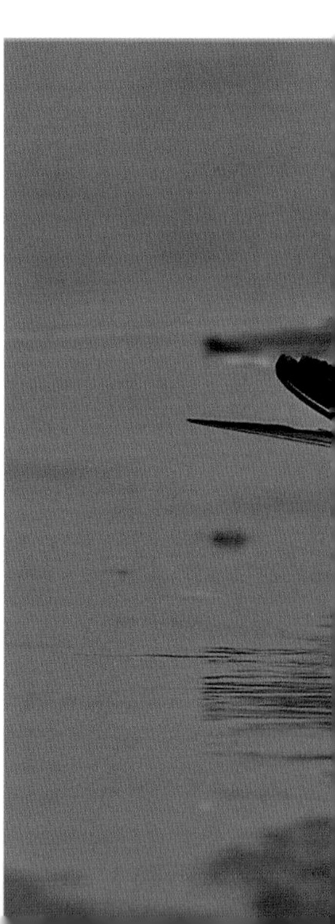

**BLACK TERN 10** Molting (alt. > basic) adult, juvenile, and immature. Aug., FL. The diversity of plumages and appearances in fall flocks of Black Terns is staggering. As Black Tern is easily identified, most of this variation is largely overlooked, but it is interesting to observe. The immature bird on the right is unusual, as it has nearly completed a molt and largely looks like a nonbreeding adult. Adult nonbreeding plumage is unlikely to be seen in North America, and the molt timing for this individual is too early for an adult. An advanced one-year-old? A two-year-old? Older? Knowledge this specialized might exist in the minds of a few individuals, or it might be entirely unknown, but, either way, it is certainly not yet widely available. The fact that pieces of information like this are still out there to be discovered is part of what makes birding continually interesting.

**BLACK TERN 11** Molting (alt. > basic) adult with Western Sandpipers. Sept., NJ. Kevin T. Karlson. Similar to the immature bird in the previous image, but the primaries are old, worn entirely black, pointing to this being an adult. The size in comparison to these Western Sandpipers really puts into context the small size of Black Terns.

**BLACK TERN 12** Breeding (alt.) adults with Least, Common, and Royal Terns. July, FL. Taking careful note of relative sizes when looking at a mixed flock is useful preparation for seeing birds far away or under difficult viewing conditions. Distinctive species like Black Tern make ideal size reference points when evaluating an unknown individual within a mixed flock. Obviously larger than the four Least Terns (at the front), obviously smaller than the Common Tern (second from the back), and far smaller than the Royal (back).

**BLACK TERN 13** Juvenile. Aug., NC. The broad wings and curved hand, as well as the dark plumage, immediately mark this as a member of the marsh tern group. The brown back and uniform wing feathers indicate that it is a juvenile. It is always good to be on the lookout for vagrants, but the gray rump confirms that this is a Black Tern, not a vagrant White-winged Tern, which have whitish rumps as juveniles.

BLACK TERN 14 Juvenile. Aug., NC. While most terns make shallow, head-first dives to grab fish and other prey just below the water, Black Tern delicately plucks prey items from the surface. Instead of a head-first, vertical dive into the water, it smoothly swoops low, barely arresting its momentum or causing a ripple on the water as it takes prey. The behavior is striking and a dead giveaway for Black Tern when seen at a distance.

BLACK TERN 15 Juvenile. Aug., NJ. Fresh juveniles show strong earthy brown fringes to the back and tertial edges, but as fall migration progresses, these fringes fade, taking on the uniformly smoky gray appearance of this individual.

BLACK TERN 16 Breeding (alt.) adult Eurasian Black Tern. May, Poland. Zbigniew Kajzer. The dark hood contrasting with the grayer body is the primary trait for separating breeding adult Eurasian Black Tern (*C. n. niger*) from breeding adult North American Black Tern, which is uniformly blackish across the head and body. The pale chin on this individual and the extreme contrast of the hood indicate that it is likely a female. Male Eurasian Black Terns show these traits more subtly.

BLACK TERN 17 Juvenile Eurasian Black Tern. Oct., France. N. J. Ransdale. The clean white flanks separate this juvenile Eurasian Black Tern from a North American Black Tern. The dark mark jutting down from the shoulder distinguishes it from a juvenile White-winged Tern.

**FLIGHT** The wingbeats are deep, with a loose quality, and in flight, this tern appears light and floating, but erratic and somewhat hesitant, since it often checks its speed slightly or bobs up or down. Black Tern lacks the power and directness seen in the flight of most terns. Still, there is a mesmerizing beauty in the Black Tern's distinctive flight. During active migration, they can move in large, loose groups, often appearing far more purposeful than when employing their usual foraging flight; there is still a bit of a slow-motion feel to the flight when compared to that of other terns.

**CALL** A quick, harsh *ker-ik* and a sharp, clear *kip*.

**RANGE** Breeds across southern Canada and the northern U.S., and in scattered pockets farther south. Widespread as a migrant, although often scarce and local, particularly in the interior and along the West Coast. Extremely rare in winter in the U.S. As a wintering species, Black Tern is primarily pelagic, with the highest concentrations in the waters from West Mexico south to Ecuador. **World:** Europe, particularly southern and eastern Europe; western and central Asia; Africa; the Caribbean; Central America; and northern South America.

**SPECIES INFO** In addition to the typical tern diet of fish, insects make up a significant portion of this species' diet and may be hawked from the air or captured terrestrially. Black Tern nests in freshwater marshes and lakes, placing its nests on mats of flattened vegetation. While the nest location can be on land, more frequently it is on vegetation that is floating in the water. As freshwater marsh is a habitat that is rapidly declining, Black Tern is showing a corresponding population decline. There are two subspecies: North American Black Tern, referable to C. *n. surinamensis*, and the nominate, *C. n. niger*, which breeds in Asia and Europe and winters primarily in western Africa, and which some taxonomic authorities split from North American Black Tern. Although it can be distinguished from *surinamensis* by subtle traits in most plumages (see final images in this account), *niger* has yet to be documented in North America, where it is likely a very rare vagrant.

**PLUMAGE INFO** In adults, the body molt overlaps broadly with both spring and fall migration, so that adults with fully black bodies are scarce away from the breeding areas. Most migrants wear a mottled mishmash of black, gray, and white feathers. In late spring and early fall, a greater percentage will display a complete or nearly complete black head and underparts, while in early spring and late fall, the reverse is true. In fall, an assortment of immature plumages are often present in areas where Black Terns gather, as are crisply marked juveniles, which, in most cases, delay their first molt until after fall migration. Because Black Tern is a very distinctive species, we sometimes overlook its variability, but that variability gives distant flocks a unique patchwork appearance. Breeding females average very slightly grayer and more matte in color tone than breeding males, but you almost need to be directly comparing a pair to detect the difference. Nominate Black Tern shows sexual plumage dimorphism more strongly.

## WHITE-WINGED TERN

*Chlidonias leucopterus*

L 9–9.5 in.; WS 22–23 in.; WT 2.1–2.8 oz.

**SIZE AND STRUCTURE** Very slightly smaller than Black Tern. Structure is quite like Black Tern, but marginally stockier with a more rounded head, a shorter, heavier bill, and longer legs. In flight, it has slightly shorter but broader wings than Black Tern. The tail is noticeably shorter than Black Tern with such a shallow notch that it appears squared off at most angles. Shows the subtly curved hand typical of all marsh terns.

**BEHAVIOR** Like Black Tern, it picks prey from the surface of the water or hawks insects from the air rather than diving for its meal like most other terns.

**FLIGHT** Flight is very similar to Black Tern, but the wings are typically held straighter, and the wingbeats are slightly stiffer. Gives a slightly more powerful impression.

**CALL** Slightly harsher and lower-pitched than Black Tern.

**RANGE** A very rare species found most regularly on the Atlantic coast, particularly in the Mid-Atlantic states. Additional eastern North American records are scattered from the Canadian Atlantic Provinces south to Georgia, with four additional records in the Great Lakes region, and one from Churchill, Manitoba. In western North America, it is accidental in western Alaska and California. **World:** Breeds from eastern Europe to northeastern China and winters from sub-Saharan Africa to Southeast Asia and Australia.

**SPECIES INFO** The wide distribution of records suggests that, while it is very rare everywhere, it is also possible anywhere. There may be fewer individuals involved than the number of records seems to indicate. It is likely that birds that are blown to this side of the Atlantic are essentially trapped here, possibly occurring in the same location in subsequent years. Hypothetically, it would be worth checking locations that have hosted White-winged Terns in prior years around the same date. There are two records of White-winged Terns pairing with Black Terns in North America—one in New York and another in Quebec. Although both nests failed, it suggests that hybrids are possible. There are no described subspecies.

**PLUMAGE INFO** Nearly all the North American records have been of adults retaining at least some breeding plumage. Adult White-winged Terns are more easily separated from Black Terns in this plumage than in other plumages, though an additional factor is that most records have been from the summer. Immature birds have occurred three times, but there are as of yet no records of juveniles. While the predominance of breeding adults is no doubt real, great scrutiny of Black Tern flocks might turn up a few immature birds and nonbreeding adults.

WHITE-WINGED TERN 1 Breeding (alt.) adults and subadult. April, Israel. Douglas Gochfeld. Just an absolutely stunning creature bound to illicit a salivary reflex in any North American birder! Unmistakable in this plumage. The duller bird on the left is a typical subadult. The shorter, heavier bill than that of Black Tern can been seen well on the center bird.

WHITE-WINGED TERN 2 Breeding (alt.) adult. April, Israel. Douglas Gochfeld. White-winged Tern is essentially just a flying field mark. Note the strongly contrasting black underwing coverts. Usually birds that are well into the molt to nonbreeding plumage will retain some of these black underwing feathers late into the year, then will attain new black underwing coverts very early the next spring. The white rump is a trait seen in all plumages, whereas Black Terns always have gray rumps.

WHITE-WINGED TERN 3 Breeding (alt.) adult. April, Poland. Scott Watson. The upper wings are much paler than those of Black Tern and contrast sharply with the black back. The wings often appear to be held straighter than those of Black Tern in flight.

WHITE-WINGED TERN 4 First-cycle. Dec., France. N. J. Ransdale. Less black on the crown than Black Tern in nonbreeding plumage. The center of the upper wing is paler than that of Black Tern, so it contrasts much more clearly with the dark leading and trailing edges of the wings, whereas Black Terns appear quite uniform. Also the rump is usually white, pale gray in this individual, not uniform with the back as in Black Tern. Finally, the outer tail feathers are usually noticeably paler than the center of the tail. Juveniles have solid brown backs, and this bird retains a few of these brown juvenile back feathers.

WHITE-WINGED TERN 5 First-cycle. Dec., France. N. J. Ransdale. First-cycle White-winged Terns lack the dark shoulder bar and the gray-washed flanks of Black Tern. The clean body should be an eye-catching trait in the field. Also notice how pudgy they appear.

**WHITE-WINGED TERN 6** Breeding (alt.) adults with Whiskered Tern. April, Ethiopia. Ken Behrens. Like Black Tern, individuals can acquire their breeding plumage on very different schedules. They are often seen with Whiskered Terns, and the difference in size is striking.

**WHITE-WINGED TERN 7** Molting (basic > alt.) adult. March, Sri Lanka. Andrew Spencer. A molting bird in early spring might slip by with a flock of Black Terns. Still, the pale upper wing should be noticeable. Also note the white rump and edges of the tail.

## WHISKERED TERN *Chlidonias hybrida*

L 9.5–10 in.; WS 26.5–28.5 in.; WT 2.9–3.2 oz.

**SIZE AND STRUCTURE** Slightly larger than Black Tern, and slightly smaller than Common Tern. Structurally distinctive, with a high, dome-shaped crown, a short but heavy bill, and a stout body. Whiskered Terns have strikingly long legs with very prominent knee joints. Side by side, they stand noticeably taller than Common or Black Tern. In flight, a Whiskered Tern can almost look like a *Sterna* tern, but has the curved hand and short tail typical of all marsh terns.

**BEHAVIOR** Like Black Tern, Whiskered Tern usually obtains prey by snatching from the surface of the water rather than diving, but occasionally does dive for prey, whereas Black Tern virtually never does; also frequently hawks flying insects on the wing. Like Black Tern, its primary habitat is freshwater, using coastal habitats only during migration.

**FLIGHT** Similar to Black Tern but steadier, more powerful, and more direct.

**CALL** A quick, dry, nasal rattle, not at all similar to other terns, somewhat frog-like or like a faster version of Green Kingfisher's flight call.

**RANGE** Three North American records, all from Cape May, NJ: July 12–15, 1993 (refound in Delaware, July 19–August 24); August 8–12, 1998; and September 12–20, 2014. There are several additional records from the Caribbean. **World:** Widespread, but patchy breeding range from southwestern Europe through eastern Asia. Winters in southern Africa through southern Asia.

**SPECIES INFO** The Latin name *hybrida* is a reference to the species' origins, as it was first described as a hybrid between Common Tern and White-winged Tern. The small number of records of this species from northern Europe and North Atlantic islands suggests that they are unlikely to come across the North Atlantic. Instead, those that end up in North America are more likely blown over the Atlantic farther south, ending up in the Caribbean or northeastern South America. They are then trapped on this side of the Atlantic, bouncing seasonally between North and South America. Vagrant White-winged Terns likely arrive in a similar manner. Three subspecies, though only the nominate, *C. h. hybrida*, has occurred in North America; the other two subspecies are found in southern Africa and Australia, respectively.

WHISKERED TERN 1 Breeding (alt.) subadult. Sept., NJ. Dustin Welch. A small but stocky tern with long legs and a short, heavy bill. Tends to hold significant amounts of breeding plumage into fall migration, and all three North American records have been on birds in nearly complete breeding plumage. Often the deep reddish legs and, occasionally, the red color of the bill are retained well into winter, and then begin to reappear early in spring, meaning that entirely black bare parts are held only briefly.

**WHISKERED TERN 2** Breeding (alt.) subadult with Common Terns and a juvenile Black Tern. Sept., NJ. Dustin Welch. While Whiskered Tern is related to Black Tern, this image makes it clear that the former is quite a different bird. The dome-shaped head and short, thick bill are reminiscent of a miniature Gull-billed Tern, and the legs are remarkably long with obvious knee joints. The white cheek stands out even more sharply than that of Arctic Tern.

**WHISKERED TERN 3** Breeding (alt.) subadult with a juvenile Black Tern. Sept., NJ. George L. Armistead/Hillstar Nature. Notice how the pale cheek stands out clearly at a distance. Patches of white nonbreeding plumage are visible on the belly, but this progresses slowly, and traces of dark gray are often retained well into winter. While the Whiskered Tern is obviously larger and broader-winged than the Black Tern, both show the wing shape typical of marsh terns with a distinctly curved hand. Whiskered Tern shows a dark trailing edge to the outer primaries like a *Sterna* tern.

WHISKERED TERN 4 Juvenile. Sept., France. N. J. Ransdale. While a full juvenile is unlikely in North America, they are quite striking. Juveniles have brown backs that are distinctly darker than the very pale wings. Unlike the solid brown back of juvenile White-winged Tern, the brown color has a broken up or faintly barred appearance. The very broad wings and short, stout bill are unique in any plumage.

WHISKERED TERN 5 Nonbreeding (basic) adult. Jan., Thailand. Jeannette Lovitch. Adults in nonbreeding plumage often show significant amounts of specking or fine streaking on the head during the winter that gives the head a distinctive grizzled appearance. This individual also still retains patches of the dark gray belly from breeding plumage. The frosty white hand is also apparent.

**PLUMAGE INFO** All records so far have been of adults retaining significant amounts of their breeding plumage, perhaps because this plumage is particularly distinctive. However, retaining breeding plumage into late fall and even some scattered feathers well into winter is typical in Whiskered Tern.

WHISKERED TERN 6 Immature (first-cycle). Jan., Sri Lanka. Ken Behrens. The head pattern of first-cycle Whiskered Terns recalls that of nonbreeding Gull-billed Terns. Notice how the back, rump, and tail are all pale gray and almost entirely uniform, unlike White-winged Tern, which shows a contrasting paler rump. By spring virtually all of the remaining dark juvenile feathers will be gone, and the upperparts will be remarkably uniform pale gray. The wing shape, almost appearing to broaden at mid-wing and remaining broad through much of the hand, is unique.

WHISKERED TERN 7 Immature (first-cycle). Jan., Thailand. Jeannette Lovitch. Whiskered Tern's build, with its strikingly heavy bill, thick neck, and long legs, recalls Gull-billed Tern, but it is actually smaller than Common Tern. The grizzled crown and nape are unique, a pattern that should immediately set off alarm bells if seen in North America. Some have paler heads with a dark streak through the eye, similar to the head pattern of nonbreeding Gull-billed Tern. In either case, the head pattern is unlike that of other marsh terns in winter. The overall color is a fairly uniform pale gray.

# PELAGIC TERNS: GENUS *ONYCHOPRION*

The word *onychoprion* is derived from combining two ancient Greek words for "claw" and "saw." One might infer that these terns' toenails have serrated edges, but it seems a myopic thing after which to name a genus. Worldwide, there are four species in the genus *Onychoprion*, three of which occur in North America. Sooty and Bridled Terns are often collectively referred to as "tropical terns," and both have extensive pantropical distributions. As breeders, though, they have only a tiny toehold in North America, reflecting the fact that this continent has only a tiny toehold on the tropics. Standing on the walls of Fort Jefferson, overlooking the Sooty Tern colony on Bush Key, it feels like a different world from the rest of North America. Perhaps even more inaccessible is the Aleutian Tern's breeding range in North America, which consists of scattered locations in western Alaska and is anything but tropical, though the species does winter in the tropical Pacific. All three species share a powerful, effortless flight style and highly contrasting plumage of grays, black, and white.

## ALEUTIAN TERN *Onychoprion aleuticus*

L 11–12 in. (tail-streamers +1.5);
WS 29.5–32 in.; WT 4.2–4.6 oz.

**SIZE AND STRUCTURE** Noticeably larger than Arctic Tern, the only tern with which it is likely to be observed. A stocky tern with a small, dome-shaped head and long wings. Shorter legs and bill than its fully tropical cousins, Bridled and Sooty Terns. While sitting, Aleutian Tern's posture appears slightly hunched forward, which causes its wings to be tilted slightly above horizontal. This appearance of holding the wings up is emphasized by a slight upward curve to the folded primaries, resulting in a resting posture that is distinctly different from that of Arctic Tern, such that the silhouettes alone are sufficient to separate these species at a distance. In flight, the wings are centered on the body, the inner wing appearing proportionally shorter and broader than that of Arctic. The hand is long and distinctly tapered, like Arctic Tern, but that of Arctic appears proportionally longer and more attenuated. Overall, its body shape is quite different from that of the tropical *Onychoprion* terns, appearing fairly short and squat in contrast to Sooty and Bridled Terns, which have long, lean bodies.

ALEUTIAN TERN 1 Breeding (alt.) adults. June, AK. Between the distinctly gray plumage, white forehead cutout, and dark trailing edge to the secondaries, Aleutian Tern is essentially a feathered field mark, particularly in its Alaskan breeding range, where Arctic Tern is the only other regular tern.

**ALEUTIAN TERN 2** Breeding (alt.) adult. June, AK. Aleutian Tern is grayer both above and below than Arctic Tern, matched only by the rare Siberian Common Tern within its North American range. The white triangular forehead cutout is similar to the related Sooty Tern, but it is completely distinctive among Alaskan terns.

**ALEUTIAN TERN 3** Breeding (alt.) adult. June, AK. Andrew Spencer. Unlike most terns, Aleutian Terns often locate their nests in grasses or sedges in the coastal tundra rather than an open beach, though they do nest on beaches in some locations.

**ALEUTIAN TERN 4** Breeding (alt.) adults. June, AK. Even grayer above than Arctic Tern. In distant, cloudy conditions, they appear particularly dark, almost blackish, though the foreheads may be visible as white flashes as they move their heads.

**ALEUTIAN TERN 5** Breeding (alt.) adult. June, AK. The triangular white cutout on the forehead is unique among terns within the North American range of Aleutian Tern, while the strong black trailing edge restricted to the secondaries is unique, period. In flight Aleutian Tern appears notably stocky, far more so than Arctic Tern.

**ALEUTIAN TERN 6** Juvenile. Aug., AK. Robin Corcoran/USFWS. The attractive juvenile plumage is rarely seen. The brown wash and gold fringes rapidly fade, though. By October, they molt into a much paler plumage that bears some similarity to an immature Common Tern.

**ALEUTIAN TERN 7** Breeding (alt.) adults. June, AK. Because of the overall dark gray color, the white leading edge of the wing really pops in the field, as does the white triangular forehead. In flight, Aleutian Tern frequently gives an odd, distinctive call that sounds like a musical House Sparrow.

**ALEUTIAN TERN 8** Breeding (alt.) adult. June, AK. The folded primaries of Aleutian Terns often appear to curve upward noticeably. This can be a simple way to separate them from Arctic Terns at great distances, as the Arctic's folded primaries are typically straighter and point straight backward.

**ALEUTIAN TERN 9** Breeding (alt.) adults. June, AK. Robin Corcoran/USFWS. Like Bridled Tern, Aleutian Tern regularly lands on floating debris when at sea. Even on a precarious perch, it keeps its wings and tail elevated in a manner unique to pelagic terns.

**ALEUTIAN TERN 10** Breeding (alt.) adults. June, AK. They appear stocky both when perched and in flight and often show a bit of a peak on the rear-crown, unlike the smoothly rounded crown of Arctic Tern, with which they are most likely to be seen.

**ALEUTIAN TERN 11** First-cycle. Dec., Australia. Hans Wohlmuth. Finding an Aleutian Tern away from the breeding ground is the Holy Grail for a West Coast birder. It has a head pattern somewhat like an immature Black Tern and body plumage more like a Common Tern, with the structure of a pelagic tern. Note that the three Aleutian Terns in the background show the oddly imbalanced posture with the wing angled upward that is typical of standing Aleutian Terns.

**BEHAVIOR** Feeds by swooping and picking from the surface rather than diving. While at sea, Aleutian Tern often rests on floating marine debris like its close relative, the Bridled Tern. Frequently nests in mixed colonies with Arctic Tern (or with Siberian Common Tern in Kamchatka, Russia) and may roost with them, but forages alone or in small flocks with other Aleutian Terns.

**FLIGHT** The wingbeats are slow and powerful, with deep strokes that strongly emphasize the downstrokes, occasionally mixing in an odd stuttering "double-flap" on the upstroke, almost giving an impression that they have been tripped in midair and are trying to regain their balance. Like other pelagic terns, Aleutian Terns often fly very high, over both land and water.

**CALL** Odd, un-tern-like musical chatter, a bit like a musical House Sparrow.

**RANGE** Local but widespread in coastal southern and western Alaska. Six records in British Columbia (five spring and one fall) are the only North American records away from the Alaskan breeding range, though there is potential for additional West Coast records. It has yet to be reported from the Hawaiian Islands. **World:** Also breeds on the Russian side of the Bering Sea. Wintering areas still being discovered, but winter records exist from the Philippines to northern Australia.

**SPECIES INFO** The records from British Columbia suggest that searching for this species in late May on the outer coast of Washington and Oregon might produce an overdue first Lower 48 record. No described subspecies.

**PLUMAGE INFO** Essentially, only adults in alternate plumage and juveniles are seen in North America, and juveniles are seen rarely, as they take to sea as soon as they fledge. Immature plumages are unrecorded on the breeding grounds, but there is much to learn about this species, and careful monitoring of gathering points near colonies in the late summer might turn up immature birds.

ALEUTIAN TERN 12 Breeding (alt.) adults. June, AK. A thick body, a neckless appearance, and broad wings create a slightly squatter, less elegant profile than most terns, particularly compared to Arctic Tern, which is the picture of slim elegance. The dark, Common Tern–like wedge on the outer primaries is another separation from Arctic Tern, as is the translucent patch on the inner primaries visible on the underwing. In Arctic Tern, the entire trailing edge of the wing shows subtle translucence, not a concentrated patch in one location.

## BRIDLED TERN *Onychoprion anaethetus*

L 12.5–14 in. (tail-streamers +2–2.5); WS 31–33.5 in.; WT 4.1–5.2 oz.

**SIZE AND STRUCTURE** Slightly smaller than Sooty Tern, about the same size as Common Tern, though the darker color usually makes it appear larger. Very similar to the structure of Sooty Tern—lean with clean lines and a flat belly, and long-tailed with a long, slim bill. In flight, the wings are long but slimmer through the inner wing than Sooty Tern, so that they appear evenly slender throughout their length, and the long, tapered hand is not as exaggerated as that of Sooty Tern. When viewed head-on, the wings appear to be held in a stronger arch than those of Sooty Tern.

**BEHAVIOR** Feeds on the creatures that take shelter amid the long lines of floating marine algae ("weeds") of the genus *Sargassum*. Frequently forages by flying slowly low over the weeds, following the path of the weed line exactly. Unlike Sooty Tern, they often alight on marine debris or even the backs of sea turtles. Because of their habitat niche, they do not usually gather in large, concentrated flocks like Sooty Terns, though they will at times join flocks of actively foraging Sooty Terns. More typically, they gather in loose groups that max out at 5–6, though singles or pairs are more frequent.

**FLIGHT** The flight appears less powerful than that of Sooty Tern, with wingbeats that are shallower, with a looser, more elastic quality compared to the deeper, more empathic wingbeats of Sooty Tern. Unlike Sooty Tern, the body bobs up and down slightly in time with the wing action, and Bridled Tern tilts and wheels frequently, adding to the impression that its flight is less stable and direct than that of Sooty Tern, and is more like the flight of Common Tern. With experience, the difference in flight style and wing structure is enough to separate Bridled from Sooty at a distance, but even without tremendous experience, Bridled stands out from Sooty Tern in direct comparison.

**RANGE** Breeds in small numbers in the Dry Tortugas of Florida, but is primarily a post-breeding visitor to the U.S., found in the Gulf of Mexico and in the warm waters of the Gulf Stream current north to the Mid-Atlantic region, occasionally as far north as the waters off Maine. In winter, a few are found in the Gulf Stream off Florida, where, at this season, they outnumber Sooty Tern. On the West Coast, Bridled Tern is a vagrant to southern California, occurring mainly in summer at tern colonies. Following tropical systems, sometimes seen from shore or even to inland bodies of water, though less frequently than Sooty Tern. **World:** Worldwide pantropical distribution.

BRIDLED TERN 1 Breeding (alt.) adult. July, FL. Trey Mitchell. A medium-sized dark, primarily pelagic tern. The black crown contrasts sharply with the gray back, and the white forehead patch is narrower than that of Sooty Tern and extends farther back past the eye.

**BRIDLED TERN 2** Breeding (alt.) adult. July, Aruba. A slender, dark tern, similar to Sooty Tern but slightly smaller and paler. The white forehead patch is longer and narrower than that of Sooty Tern, while the black line through the eye is typically broader. Note how the pale vanes extending into the dark trailing edge of the primaries on the opposite wing blunt the contrast between the dark primaries and the white underwing coverts.

**BRIDLED TERN 3** Breeding (alt.) adult. July, FL. Trey Mitchell. Depending on the angle, the whitish collar can be obvious or very difficult to see. The black crown contrasts strongly with the back, while this contrast on Sooty Tern is less apparent because the back is much darker. The entire outermost tail feathers are completely white, and sometimes the adjacent tail feathers are as well. In Sooty Tern only the outer webs of the outer tail feathers are white. This exact pattern is very difficult to judge under field conditions, but the result is that the white along the edges of the tail is more visible in Bridled Tern.

**BRIDLED TERN 4** Breeding (alt.) Bridled Tern (left) and Sooty Tern (right) comparison. July, Aruba/Aug., NC. The difference in the shape of the forehead patch is obvious at close range—that of Bridled Tern is narrower and has a shape reminiscent of an eyebrow, extending behind the eye, while the broader white patch of Sooty Tern extends only to the midpoint of the eye. The black crown contrasts with the back on Bridled Tern, while Sooty Tern shows little to no contrast.

**BRIDLED TERN 5** Breeding (alt.) adult. July, Aruba. The white forehead patch is narrow and creates the appearance of a white eyebrow, completely unlike the short, fat forehead patch of Sooty Tern.

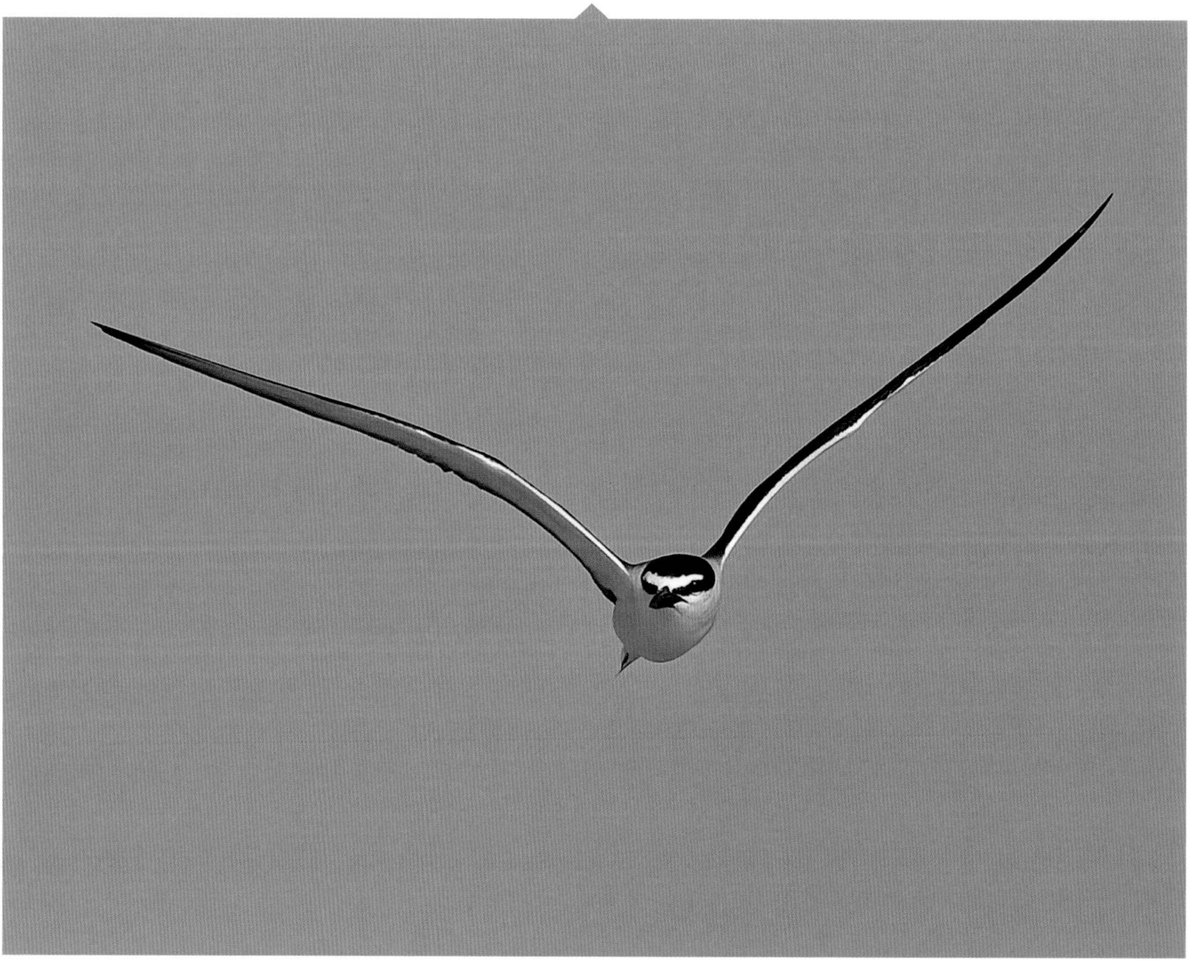

BRIDLED TERN 6 Breeding (alt.) adult and juvenile. June, Mexico. L. Guillermo. Unlike Sooty Terns, Bridled Terns nest in small, loose colonies, placing their nests in sheltered crevasses. Notice the mottled appearance of the adult; Bridled Terns begin their molt to nonbreeding during the breeding season. Note also the shadow of the adult eyebrow on the juvenile and its extensive pale back.

BRIDLED TERN 7 Juvenile. Aug., NC. Juvenile Bridled Terns have broad, pale hind-collars and gray mantles liberally fringed with white, as well as pale heads. This combination is quite unique and utterly unlike juvenile Sooty Terns. The difference in tail length is dramatic in juveniles as well, with Bridled Terns having much longer tails at this age.

**BRIDLED TERN 8** Juvenile. Aug., NC. When coming straight at you, the pale heads of juveniles often gleam white, contrasting with the slate gray wings, making the identification simple. Like many adults, juveniles have backs that are paler than the wings, immediately separating them from Sooty Tern.

**BRIDLED TERN 9** Juvenile and breeding (alt.) adult. Aug., NC. Juveniles stay close to their parents for several months after fledging. Juvenile Bridled Terns often appear white-headed at a distance, a very distinctive trait, and if a white-headed juvenile is associating with an adult tropical tern, it is a very good bet that the adult is also a Bridled. All ages show strong white vanes to the undersides of the primaries.

**BRIDLED TERN 10** Immatures. Sept., FL. Reinhard Geisler. While not as white-headed as juveniles, immature and nonbreeding adult Bridled Terns have predominately white heads, unlike Sooty Tern, and this is a better trait for identification at a distance than the details of head pattern. The back is paler than the wings, which is never the case for Sooty Tern. Immatures also tend to show more obvious pale hind-collars than adults.

**BRIDLED TERN 11** Immature. Sept., FL. Reinhard Geisler. Immatures and nonbreeding adults are very similar, particularly the head pattern, which is heavily flecked with white but retains much of the distinctive shape of the white forehead patch. The brown tinge to the coverts marks this as an immature bird. Unlike Sooty Terns, Bridled Terns often perch on marine debris, but never land on the ocean, which Sooty Terns do on occasion.

**BRIDLED TERN 12** Breeding (alt.) adults. April, FL. Douglas Gochfeld. The breeding displays of terns are given frequently and are a joy to observe. The white eyebrow is distinctive from both angles but does give a different impression when viewed head-on versus from the side. Also note the sharp division between the black head and pale upper back.

**BRIDLED TERN 13** Comparison between breeding (alt.) adult Bridled (left) and Sooty (right) Terns. Left image June, FL. Trey Mitchell. Right image Aug., NC. Note how the pale vanes on the undersides of the primaries on the Bridled Tern cause the pale underwing to appear to bleed into the wingtip. On the Sooty Tern there is a solidly dark wingtip and a crisp division between the primaries and underwing coverts. This trait is often the best for separating these two species at a distance.

**BRIDLED TERN 14** Immature (first-cycle). Jan., FL. Floating seaweed known as *Sargassum* is the favorite habitat of Bridled Tern. Many species of fish and other marine life use these weed mats for shelter, and Bridled Terns hunt along long lines of weed, resting on floating debris when it is available. Tropical terns are scarce in winter north of the Caribbean, but Bridled Tern is far more likely than Sooty Tern, and most such Bridleds will be immature birds.

**BRIDLED TERN 15** Immature (first-cycle). May, FL. Dan Irizarry. Worn first-cycle birds can be nearly as white-headed as juveniles and often are quite pale-backed. The largely pale tail is longer than that of immature Sooty Terns, but this distinction is difficult to see at a distance.

**BRIDLED TERN 16** Subadult. Aug., NC. Ken Behrens. The largely pale head and pale vanes on the undersides of the primaries make the identification straightforward. The wings are slimmer at the base than those of Sooty Tern. The dark oval is an incoming outer primary; missing or growing primaries, particularly outer primaries, affect wing shape and, to some degree, flight style in late summer.

**CALL** Usually silent away from breeding areas. Adults make a yelping *Wek* similar to a Black-necked Stilt or a soft Black Skimmer; also an extended low chuckle. Juveniles make an incessant peeping call as they follow their parent, begging for several months after fledging.

**SPECIES INFO** Almost entirely pelagic away from the breeding grounds. Immature Bridled Terns often outnumber adults in the Gulf Stream off the eastern U.S., while the same pattern is never true of Sooty Tern. Immature Sooty Terns are thought to leave the region entirely after they become independent from their parents, while it seems that immature Bridled Terns readily wander the Gulf Stream during the period before they begin breeding. Subspecies are slightly to moderately well defined over Bridled Tern's extensive global range, with 4–6 subspecies recognized. The two subspecies that occur in North America—*O. a. melanoptera*, the subspecies breeding in the Dry Tortugas and the source of most eastern U.S. records; and *O. a. nelsoni*, the likely subspecies of southern California vagrants—are quite similar.

**PLUMAGE INFO** Unlike Sooty Tern, many of the Bridled Terns seen in North America are immature birds and are very similar to nonbreeding adults. Full breeding plumage adults are also frequently observed, particularly in spring through late summer. Juvenile plumage can be seen at sea from late summer and well into fall, usually in the company of adults.

## SOOTY TERN *Onychoprion fuscatus*

L 14–15.5 in. (tail-streamers +2.5–3);
WS 34–36.5 in.; WT 6.3–7.2 oz.

**SIZE AND STRUCTURE** Larger and broader-winged than Common Tern and Bridled Tern, about the same size as Sandwich Tern, but longer-winged and appearing larger due to its dark color and slightly heavier build. Sooty Tern has a lean but athletic appearance, with slight expansion at the chest, a long, forked tail, a small head, and a long, slender bill. The wings are set forward of center on the body and are moderately broad-based, while the hand is exceptionally long and tapered.

**BEHAVIOR** Forages frequently in flocks, sometimes quite large flocks, while, within North America, Bridled Tern is more often found individually, in pairs, or in small flocks. Feeds primarily on schools of small fish driven to the surface by larger predatory fish. Usually snatches prey directly from the surface or makes very shallow dives from a short distance above the water, never completely submerging its body. Unlike Bridled Tern, it rarely perches on floating debris while at sea, though Sooty Tern will, occasionally, rest on the surface of the ocean, something Bridled Tern does not do. Looks awkward floating, with folded wings and tail angled upward sharply to keep them dry. Frequently flies at great heights while at sea, unlike Bridled, and sometimes in small, swirling flocks that are reminiscent of a kettle of migrating raptors or distant frigatebirds.

**FLIGHT** Direct and powerful with quick, deep, crisp downstroke, while the upstroke flies up loosely, in windy conditions or at sea. On the breeding grounds or when flying high, the flight is less purposeful and much more buoyant, with shallower wingbeats.

**CALL** An odd, nasal, two-parted squeak, *Wecka-wack*, given constantly around the breeding grounds and occasionally at sea, particularly when flocks are actively foraging over a school of fish. Juveniles give a begging call while following their parents for several months after fledging that is more strident and sharper than the begging call of Bridled Tern, recalling the begging call of Royal Tern.

SOOTY TERN 1 Breeding (alt.) adult. April, FL. John Groskopf. A medium-sized tern with a lean build, garbed in strongly contrasting black and white. The bill is long and thin but heavier than that of Bridled Tern. The white forehead extends backward only to the eye.

SOOTY TERN 2 Breeding (alt.) adult. June, FL. Tammy McQuade. The white forehead patch is bold and obvious when observed head-on, similar in shape to the pale forehead of a Cliff Swallow, but the corners do not extend behind the eye. In contrast, the white forehead of Bridled Tern is much narrower when viewed head-on but extends farther behind the eye, giving it the appearance of a white eyebrow, and is more easily seen from the side.

SOOTY TERN 3 Breeding (alt.) adult. April, FL. Daniel Irons. The upperparts are uniformly dark. There is little contrast between the black cap and upper back, the mantle and wings are identical, and the white in the tail is limited to the outer webs of the outermost tail feathers and disappears at any distance. Sooty Tern's dynamic flight style includes frequent banking and as it tilts toward you this uniformity immediately separates Sooty from Bridled Tern.

SOOTY TERN 4 Breeding (alt.) adults and juveniles. June, Mexico. L. Guillermo. In bright sunlight, the adult's back can appear brownish, recalling Bridled Tern, but the color is uniform across the wings and back, whereas Bridled has a distinctly paler back. Sooty Terns are one of the most abundant seabirds in the world, with a total population that may exceed 50 million. Sooty Tern colonies are often massive and tightly packed, with pairs occupying every available inch of real estate.

SOOTY TERN 5 Breeding (alt.) adults. Aug., NC. Sooty Tern feeds on small baitfish driven to the surface by larger predatory fish, particularly small flying fish being attacked by tuna. It usually picks food directly from the surface; it dives infrequently and from only a short distance above the surface. Notice the limited amount of white in the outer tail.

SOOTY TERN 6 Juvenile. Aug., NC. The dark juvenile plumage is quite distinct from other terns, though the pale underwing coverts and undertail coverts are fairly muted, so they contrast very little and are far less apparent at a distance than the bright white underwings of adults. At times, Sooty Tern appears completely dark at a distance, creating the potential for confusion with noddies. Note how the inner wing is fairly broad, broader than that of Bridled Tern, while the hand is exceptionally long and tapered, with a straight leading edge that imparts an angular appearance.

SOOTY TERN 7 Juvenile. Feb., Australia. Hans Wohlmuth. The dark juvenile is so unique that it can really only be confused with a noddy or a dark jaeger. They are longer-winged than noddies, with a more pointed hand, a narrower, forked tail, and faster, snappier wingbeats. Jaegers are more compact, with a larger head and an even faster, more purposeful flight. Unlike that of a jaeger or a noddy, the underwing of Sooty Tern flashes pale with every upstroke when well lit. Be aware that Black Terns can be quite pelagic in the winter and during migration. While you are unlikely to mistake a Sooty Tern for a Black Tern, assuming that all dark terns in pelagic waters are Sooty Terns can result in mistaking a Black Tern for a Sooty, though they are unalike in size, flight style, and plumage.

SOOTY TERN 8 Breeding (alt.) adult. April, FL. Daniel Irons. Sooty Tern is broad-winged and has a powerfully built body for its size, but is quite small-headed, which causes the long bill to be more noticeable. Note how the tail-streamer has white only on the outer web, while the inner web has a dark band; in Bridled Tern the entire outermost tail feather is white.

SOOTY TERN 9 Breeding (alt.) adult. Aug., NC. The jet-black undersides of the primaries contrast distinctly with the white underwing coverts, creating a two-toned underwing where the divisions between light and dark are stark and discernable even at a distance. In Bridled Tern pale vanes extend from the white underwing coverts into the primaries, blurring the division between light and dark.

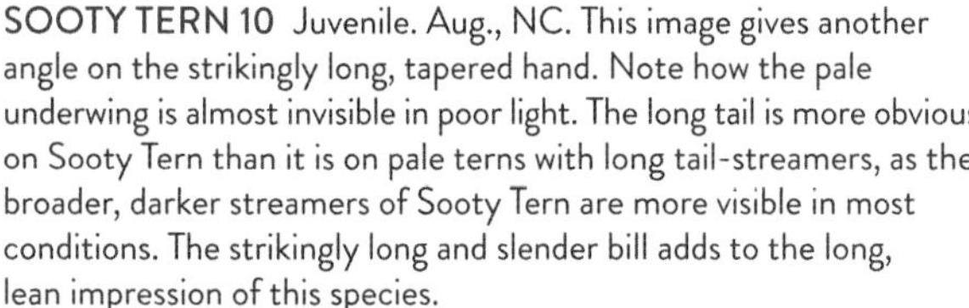

**SOOTY TERN 10** Juvenile. Aug., NC. This image gives another angle on the strikingly long, tapered hand. Note how the pale underwing is almost invisible in poor light. The long tail is more obvious on Sooty Tern than it is on pale terns with long tail-streamers, as the broader, darker streamers of Sooty Tern are more visible in most conditions. The strikingly long and slender bill adds to the long, lean impression of this species.

**SOOTY TERN 11** Breeding (alt.) adult. Aug., NC. The sharp demarcation between the white underwing coverts and the black undersides of the flight feathers is often the most useful plumage trait for separating Sooty Tern from Bridled Tern at moderate to long distances. Better known traits, such as the amount of white in the tail and the shape of the white patch on the forehead, are often far more difficult to discern on distant birds.

**SOOTY TERN 12** Breeding (alt.) adults with Audubon's Shearwaters. Aug., NC. Note how the stark division of black and white on the underwing stands out clearly, even at a distance. When approaching a feeding flock that includes tropical terns, should you see splashes and fish jumping on the surface but no distinct brownish-orange patches of *Sargassum* weed, chances are strong that the tropical terns will be Sooty Terns. If it is a small flock and lots of *Sargassum* is present, then the associated tropical terns are more likely to be Bridled Terns.

SOOTY TERN 13 Breeding (alt.) adult. April, FL. Daniel Irons. Sooty Tern flight is direct, with a purposeful appearance that is somewhat like that of a jaeger. Wingbeats are snappy and deep. These flight style tendencies can be effective for distant identification, but the long, angular wings that taper to a particularly sharply pointed wingtip and the distinctly two-toned underwings will also greatly improve the accuracy of distant identifications.

SOOTY TERN 14 Adult, juvenile, and immature. Sept., FL. Paul Mason. Sooty Tern is a lightweight seabird that often soars high in the air and is therefore particularly prone to being displaced by hurricanes. This image was taken after the passage of Hurricane Sally. The bird on the right is an immature bird, likely just over a year old, while the bird in the center is a fresh juvenile. The immature bird is interesting, as this is a rare plumage in North America. Most immature Sooty Terns are thought to spend several years in the waters off western Africa and are entirely pelagic during that period, only returning when ready to breed. For that reason, there is not much information about the plumage progression in Sooty Tern, but this immature is likely to be molting into a plumage that is adult-like, but with a messy, dark mottled appearance, apparently the typical progression after the juvenile-like plumages.

**RANGE** The only major breeding colony in the United States is in Florida, on Bush Key, in the Dry Tortugas. Sooty Tern occasionally breeds in small numbers amid large tern colonies at scattered locations along the Gulf Coast, usually only 1–3 pairs at any one location. Away from the breeding grounds, Sooty Tern is found in the warm offshore waters of the Gulf of Mexico, and even more frequently in the Gulf Stream current north to North Carolina. It is rare farther north in the Gulf Stream; rare but regular in coastal locations in the Mid-Atlantic and even New England after tropical systems; and more rare in inland rivers and lakes, including the eastern Great Lakes, after particularly large storms. Sooty Tern is occasionally displaced even farther by storms, and there are records from nearly all eastern states and Atlantic Canada, as well as western locations like West Texas, New Mexico, and Colorado. It is extremely rare to find Sooty Tern off California and north to Alaska. **World:** Abundant pantropical distribution.

**SPECIES INFO** Almost entirely pelagic away from the breeding grounds. Because of this, it is a difficult species to observe in most of North America, though it is one of the most abundant seabirds globally, breeding in vast colonies in tropical regions throughout the world. There are seven described subspecies, though they are weakly differentiated and questions remain as to the accuracy of the current taxonomic picture. The nominate subspecies, *O. f. fuscatus*, breeding in the Caribbean, is the subspecies observed in eastern North America, while California records likely pertain to *O. f. crissalis*, and the subspecies breeding in Hawaii is *O. f. oahuensis*.

**PLUMAGE INFO** Adults show little seasonal change; away from the breeding season, they have slight white flecking on the head, and on some birds, the head is tinged with brown rather than showing the jet-black facial pattern of the breeding season. Juvenile plumage is seen frequently among flocks of Sooty Terns in warm Gulf Stream waters. There is some confusion about plumage progression in this species between juvenile and adult plumage, in part because immature birds are entirely pelagic for several years. After juvenile plumage, their appearance for their first summer into fall, when they are over a year old, looks like a messier version of their juvenile plumage, often with some pale patches on the belly and a faint pale forehead. Then they acquire a subadult plumage nearly identical to adult plumage, but with smudges of gray or brown on the underparts and scattered pale flecking on the head.

SOOTY TERN 15 Breeding (alt.) adults. May, FL. John Groskopf. Terns tend to avoid landing on the water because they lack the waterproofing of gulls, but Sooty Terns do land on the water rarely. When they do, they adopt this odd posture, keeping all their flight feathers as far from the water as possible. Their small-headed appearance is far more evident from a distance than it is when viewing nearby Sooty Terns.

# NODDIES: GENUS *ANOUS*

The word *anous* is simply the ancient Greek word for "foolish" or "without understanding." Worldwide, there are five currently recognized species in the genus *Anous*, one of which is regular in North America, and another occurs as a vagrant. Their dark bodies and pale caps make them look completely different from most terns. In all likelihood, they are not terns. They differ from terns in many aspects of life history, including building elaborate nests, feeding by landing in the water to seize prey rather than diving, and paddling their feet on the surface of the water like storm-petrels. Studies have suggested that, like skimmers that are in their own subfamily apart from terns, noddies also are distinct from terns genetically.

## BROWN NODDY *Anous stolidus*

L 14–16 in.; WS 31–35 in.; WT 5–7.7 oz.

**SIZE AND STRUCTURE** Nearly identical in dimensions to Sooty and Sandwich Terns, though it appears bulkier than both. Notably smaller and shorter-winged than any of the jaegers, with which it can be confused when seen poorly at sea. Sitting, it has a balanced, well-portioned appearance, not as attenuated as most terns with a smallish head and long, fairly heavy bill. In flight, its structure is less unassuming. The body is lean but heavy-chested and the wings are proportionally shorter and broader-based than most terns, with blunter tips. The long tail is usually held closed when in flight, creating the appearance of a spike-like trailing projection, but is strikingly broad and graduated when open, usually when landing, hovering, or making a dramatic change of direction.

BROWN NODDY 1 Adult. April, FL. With a pale cap and dark body, the overall appearance is the reverse of most terns. Among terns it can only be confused with its close relative, Black Noddy, which is much rarer than Brown Noddy. The cap merges gradually with the nape, the bill is stout, and the body is warm brown, all traits that separate it from Black Noddy.

BROWN NODDY 2 Adult. April, FL. The bill is long but relatively broad-based and expands noticeably at the midpoint, adding to the heavy-billed impression. The white crown gradually fades into the brown nape with no clear line of delineation, unlike Black Noddy. The ring underneath the eye extends farther forward than that of Black Noddy, wrapping around in front of the eye, while it usually only reaches the midpoint of the eye in Black Noddy.

**BEHAVIOR** The name "noddy" comes from these birds' courtship displays, which involve bowing and nodding between the male and female. They often perch on buoys, oil drilling rigs, and other offshore structures, both floating and stationary. Around breeding areas, they regularly perch on scrubby trees, and even often place their nests in trees. Their feeding behavior far less graceful than more terns, hovering just above the water and seizing prey from the surface, paddling their feet in the water, and even splashing their bellies into the water, but not plunge-diving.

**FLIGHT** Direct and powerful, usually close to the surface of the water. The wingbeats are rather shallow, slower and looser than Sooty Tern, with a somewhat gull-like appearance. Brown Noddy rocks side to side sometimes, though not as regularly as Sooty and Bridled Terns. In strong winds, they make some use of the active soaring flight technique most common in tubenoses, setting their wings and arcing up and down. This is extremely rare in other terns, and could cause confusion with other dark, pelagic seabirds, such as dark shearwaters and jaegers. Noddies are generally less proficient than these species at this flight style and make shorter, lower arcs.

**CALL** A variety of harsh croaks on the breeding grounds, but generally silent away from the breeding grounds.

**BROWN NODDY 3** Adults. July, Aruba. The typical breeding habitat for Brown Noddies in the Caribbean. The bird coming in to land displays the full wedge-shaped tail, usually held close except when changing direction or landing. Also note the small-headed appearance of the bird perched up high, imparting a pigeon-like appearance unique to noddies.

**BROWN NODDY 4** Adults, juvenile, and immature. July, Aruba. Within the U.S., breeds only at Bush Key in the Dry Tortugas, Florida, but also breeds widely in the Caribbean. The warm tones to the plumage and robust bodies eliminate Black Noddy. Even at a distance the white cap appears to fade into the dark body with no sharp lines of delineation. Those with more limited white are immatures, while the extensively white-headed birds are adults.

**RANGE** Breeds only on Bush Key in the Dry Tortugas in the Florida Keys, where abundant; rare elsewhere in South Florida; and exceptional or very rare in the Gulf of Mexico and along the southern Atlantic coast. Occasionally found outside normal range after hurricanes, though far less frequently than Sooty Tern. **World:** Abundant pantropical distribution.

**SPECIES INFO** The species has one of the most insulting scientific names, *Anous*, meaning "without understanding" in Greek, and *stolidus*, meaning "slow of mind" in Latin. They were easy to approach and hunt when Europeans first came in contact with them, but nevertheless, the multi-language insult seems excessive. There are 4–5 subspecies described, depending on which taxonomic authority is followed; *A. s. stolidus* is the subspecies found in eastern North America. There is a possibility that one or more of the currently recognized subspecies may eventually attain species status, particularly the very dark birds from the Galapagos, *A. s. galapagensis*.

**PLUMAGE INFO** Noddies are the only terns that show almost no seasonal or age-related differences in plumage. First-cycle birds have slightly less white on the crown and have different molt timing, but are otherwise similar to adults.

BROWN NODDY 5 Adult. April, FL. The warm tones to the body are indicative of Brown Noddy; Black Noddy always appears cold-toned. Noddies as a group have very distinctively shaped tails, but as they hold their tails closed except when hovering or landing (as this bird is doing) it is usually difficult to fully appreciate the odd, graduated tail shape. The wings are also comparatively shorter, slightly broader, and with blunter tips than typical terns.

**BROWN NODDY 6** Adults. July, Aruba. While it also stands on sandy beaches, Brown Noddy is far more prone to perch on structures than other terns. Notice the less attenuated appearance compared with most terns and that the wingtips and tip of the tail are equal in length.

**BROWN NODDY 7** Immature. April, FL. Immature noddies are similar to adults, but notice the pale cap is far less extensive, the wing coverts appear battered, and it is replacing primaries in spring, when only immature birds are in molt. In some individuals the reduced cap is also more sharply defined than that of adults, appearing more similar to Black Noddy. However, they tend to be even warmer brown than adults, and thus less like Black Noddy in this highly useful trait.

**BROWN NODDY 8** Immature. April, FL. On Brown Noddies in their first spring the white on the head is concentrated on the forecrown and they have obvious new inner primaries and worn retained juvenile outers. At first glance, the cap of this Brown Noddy has similarities to the pattern of the pale cap on Black Noddies. Viewed more closely, the rear border of the cap bleeds gradually into the nape rather than showing a clear line of demarcation. Additionally, the bill is stout, and there are obvious warm brown tones to the body plumage.

BROWN NODDY 9 Adult. July, Aruba. The warm tones to the plumage are typical of Brown Noddy but never present on Black Noddy. The strong contrast created between the blackish secondaries and the warm-toned wing coverts is another Brown Noddy trait, as Black Noddy shows little to no contrast between these areas. Brown Noddies also have slightly broader inner wings and shorter, blunter hands compared to other terns, so the wing silhouette is a bit like that of a medium-sized gull.

BROWN NODDY 10 Adult. July, Aruba. In high winds, they may arc over the waves on set wings in the manner of shearwaters. They don't quite have the gliding chops to be confused with a shearwater for more than a moment or two, though. Their glides are short and punctuated by obvious tern-like wing flaps, which in high wind are much deeper than the typical wingbeat. A distant noddy could also briefly be confused for a dark-morph jaeger. However, noddies lack the jaegers' easy power, and their wingbeats are deeper and floppier than the jaegers' quick, crisp strokes.

**BROWN NODDY 11** Juvenile and adult. July, Aruba. The uniform wing coverts and fresh primaries lacking any molt limits indicate that this bird is a juvenile. Noddies show very little age-related or seasonal change, so the pattern of the crown and the degree of molt and wear are the traits used to age these birds. To identify this Brown Noddy, note the stout bill and the white ring under the eye that extends beyond the midpoint of the eye.

**BROWN NODDY 12** Adult. July, Aruba. The tail is usually closed in flight and has the appearance of a long, substantial spike. Among North American terns, only the two noddies have this trait, and Brown Noddy has a longer tail than Black Noddy. The broad wings, slight expansion at the chest, heavy bill, and warm brown tones to the plumage also distinguish it from Black Noddy. It flies strongly and directly, typically very low over the water.

## BLACK NODDY *Anous minutus*

L 12–13.5 in.; WS 26–29 in.; WT 3.2–4 oz.

**SIZE AND STRUCTURE** Very similar in size to Common Tern, significantly smaller than Sandwich Tern, and strikingly smaller than Brown Noddy. It has a much slimmer appearance than Brown Noddy, with a significantly less bulky body, a long neck, a small, rounded head, and a straight bill that is oddly long and very slender. The length of the bill is clearly greater than the length of the head; Brown Noddy has a 1:1 head-to-bill ratio, while the difference in the depth of the bill between the two noddies is even more striking. The legs are short, proportionally shorter than Brown Noddy, and are centered on the body.

**BEHAVIOR** Like Brown Noddy, it prefers to use high perches when it can. It has an even stronger tendency than Brown Noddy to land on boats and to briefly land on the ocean. Like other terns, it will make quick surface dives to catch prey, but the usual feeding method is hovering barely above the water, pattering its feet on the water, and snapping up prey from this position.

**FLIGHT** Flies strongly and directly, usually very close to the surface of the water. The wingbeats are quick and agile.

**CALL** A variety of croaks and rattles, but unlikely to be heard away from the breeding grounds.

**RANGE** Rare. Most years 1–2 can be found associating with the large Brown Noddy colony in the Dry Tortugas, in the Florida Keys. The highest number from a single year in the Tortugas was five, though in other years they may be absent. Away from the Dry Tortugas, there is one record from the Tampa Bay area and two records from the Texas coast. **World:** Pantropical, but far more abundant in the Pacific than the Atlantic, and absent from the Indian Ocean.

**SPECIES INFO** Seven described subspecies. The Dry Tortugas birds most likely are subspecies *A. m. americanus* of the Caribbean, though the original Florida specimen was said to have been definitively identified as *A. m. atlanticus* (Robertson et al. 1961), the tropical Atlantic Ocean subspecies. There are four Pacific subspecies that differ only slightly from the Atlantic subspecies in measurements, the extent of the pale cap, a paler tail, or paler feet. The fifth Pacific subspecies, the Hawaiian Noddy, *A. m. melanogenys*, is quite scarce, numbering only about 2000 pairs. It has an extensively frosty gray head and tail and orange feet, and differs significantly from other Black Noddy subspecies.

**PLUMAGE INFO** Most seen in the U.S. are immature birds, often showing extremely worn wing coverts, but adults have been seen on occasion as well. The differences between adults and immature birds are not striking, though immature birds show less extensive, more sharply defined white caps than adults.

BLACK NODDY 1 Adult. Nov., French Polynesia. Jean Iron. Strikingly slender overall with a small head and extraordinarily long bill. The entire structure is a field mark, but the body is darker than Brown Noddy and cold-toned. The white under-eye arc barely extends past the midpoint of the eye, unlike Brown Noddy, whose arc wraps in front of the eye.

**BLACK NODDY 2** Immature with Brown Noddy. June, FL. Tammy McQuade. Unmistakably smaller overall in direct comparison to Brown Noddy. Slender-billed and small-headed. Strong sunlight can cause the blackish color to appear bleached out, but they always appear cold-toned compared to the warmer tones of Brown Noddy.

**BLACK NODDY 3** Immature with Brown Noddy. June, FL. Tammy McQuade. The bill is so long and slender it almost has a comical appearance. The very sharply defined crown indicates that this is an immature bird, as are most that occur in the Dry Tortugas. The cold blackish color is also distinctive when compared directly to Brown Noddy.

BLACK NODDY 4 Adult. June, Mexico. L. Guillermo. The bill is both strikingly long and narrow, and of fairly even depth throughout its length, not distinctly deeper at the base like that of Brown Noddy. The bill is longer than the length of the head. The pale crown is less clearly defined than that of immature birds, blending into the nape.

BLACK NODDY 5 Immature. June, FL. Tammy McQuade. Notice how the bill is of nearly even width throughout its length so it has a peg-like appearance. The under-eye arc only extends forward to the midpoint of the eye. The brown blur in the background is a Brown Noddy, which gives a good feel for the difference in color between the two species.

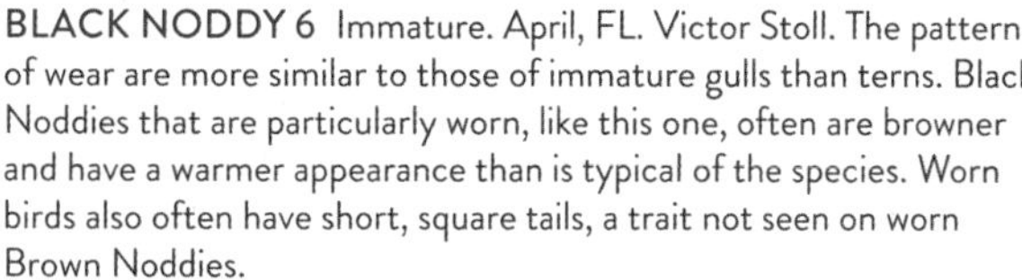

**BLACK NODDY 6** Immature. April, FL. Victor Stoll. The patterns of wear are more similar to those of immature gulls than terns. Black Noddies that are particularly worn, like this one, often are browner and have a warmer appearance than is typical of the species. Worn birds also often have short, square tails, a trait not seen on worn Brown Noddies.

**BLACK NODDY 7** Immature. April, FL. Douglas Gochfeld. The sharply defined white cap is particularly noticeable on this individual. Also note the slender bill, small head, and slender neck.

**BLACK NODDY 8** Immature. April, FL. Douglas Gochfeld. The heavy wing molt at this time of year indicates that this is an immature bird and is likely to have at least some effect on the flight style of this individual. Heavily worn immature Black Noddies often have a hint of a warm tone to the plumage a bit like Brown Noddy, but note the long, slender bill, clearly defined cap, and blackish neck.

# SKIMMERS: GENUS *RYNCHOPS*

This genus was originally named by Linnaeus, though he somehow mistranslated the Greek root word he was intending to use; while he apparently intended the name to mean "beak-face," when he originally published the name, the spelling he used actually meant "cutoff bill," an excellent reference to the maxilla. Naming all of the species in the known world has never seemed so relatable. There are three currently recognized species of skimmers in the world, but only Black Skimmer occurs in North America. Skimmers are currently placed in Rynchopinae, a subfamily of the family Laridae. By current taxonomic understanding, Laridae is made up of three sub-groups: gulls, terns, and skimmers. So while Rynchopinae is a much smaller group than gulls or terns, skimmers are quite distinct and given equal status with these groups. Finding the correct taxonomic placement for skimmers has been a circuitous process that may not be at an end. They have previously been considered part of terns, are more closely related to gulls, and treated by some authors as their own distinct family. This is unsurprising given their unusual behavior and characteristics. Their unique feeding style is facilitated by two specific traits: they are the only birds in the world that have a lower mandible that juts out past the upper mandible; they also have vertical, cat-like pupils, which allows them to see well enough to forage day or night, as their preferred tidal conditions shift. Black Skimmer is the only skimmer that is a coastal species; the other two skimmers, Indian Skimmer and African Skimmer, make sandy islands within rivers their primary habitat.

## BLACK SKIMMER *Rynchops niger*

L 17–18 in.; WS 45–49 in.; WT 9–13 oz.

**SIZE AND STRUCTURE** Utterly distinctive. Size is similar to Royal Tern, but slightly slimmer. Short legs give Black Skimmer a low-slung appearance when standing, and the long wings exaggerate the attenuation of the body, like an extra-long ice cream cone set on its side. The bill is strikingly long and distinctively shaped, with the lower mandible extending beyond the upper mandible, a trait found only in skimmers. In flight, the long, angular wings are swept back at the wrist, and the long bill juts down at an angle below the body.

**BEHAVIOR** Foraging Black Skimmers fly just above the surface of the water and use their unique elongated lower mandibles to slice through the water, foraging by touch. When the lower mandible touches a fish, the upper mandible snaps down, snagging the fish like a mouse trap. Most often, skimmers feed individually, but they also feed cooperatively in pairs, or, more rarely, in small groups. At dusk, groups of Black Skimmers will often form densely packed flocks that sally out over water, and spend several minutes performing series after series of tight turns and undulations in perfect synchrony, appearing almost like a flock of sandpipers evading a falcon.

**FLIGHT** The wingbeats are distinctively slow and stately, often appearing nearly in slow motion. Their wing action is particularly distinctive, with the upstroke extending high above the body, while the downstroke stops level with the plane of the body. This combination is diagnostic; the shallow downstroke allows them to fly close to the surface without dragging their wingtips in the water.

**CALL** A far-carrying *yip-yip* or *yap-yap* with a distinctive barking quality. Its unique call echoing through the darkness is a characteristic nocturnal sound of coastal estuaries.

**RANGE** Almost entirely coastal. Year-round on the Gulf Coast, southern California, and on the southern Atlantic coast to northern South Carolina, while along the Atlantic they breed north to Massachusetts, vacating New England and the Mid-Atlantic for the winter. Rarely wanders north as far as Newfoundland in the East, and very rarely to Oregon in the West. **World:** Widespread in Central and South America.

**SPECIES INFO** Skimmers have vertical pupils like a cat, giving them excellent night vision, which allows them to feed on favorable tidal conditions no matter the time of day or night. Unlike terns, the sexes can be easily distinguished in Black Skimmer. Males have much larger bodies, broader wings, and longer and deeper-based bills. In direct comparison, females are clearly smaller and slimmer. Females' bills are slimmer-based and distinctly shorter overall, and the distance that the lower mandible extends past the upper mandible is also shorter. An additional difference is that the base of the bill in males is usually a slightly washed-out orange-red color, while in females the base of the bill tends to be a more intense, reddish color, though there is some overlap. There are three subspecies; only the nominate, *R. n. niger*, occurs

**BLACK SKIMMER 1** Breeding (alt.) adult. Aug., NJ. Jesse Amesbury. A spectacular creature with a unique bill that it uses to slice through the surface of the water foraging for small fish. The striking plumage, distinctive shape, and unusual behavior make Black Skimmer one of the most unique and distinctive bird species in North America.

**BLACK SKIMMER 2** Breeding (alt.) adult with chick. Aug., NJ. Jesse Amesbury. The lower mandible is significantly longer than the upper. The world's three species of skimmers are the only birds that possess this trait. The transformation that the bills of baby skimmers undergo in a few months is extraordinary. Recently hatched birds have short, round bills, similar to those of fledgling large terns, better for handling the fish adults bring to them. They become independent with bills that still are only two-thirds of the length of adults', and their bills continue to grow slowly, taking 5–6 months to reach adult length.

in North America, while the other two, *R. n. cinerascens* and *R. n. intercedens*, are found in South America. The Amazonian subspecies, *R. n. cinerascens*, is larger than the nominate subspecies and has a distinctive dusky underwing, an almost entirely black tail, and a narrower white secondary border; it performs significant migratory movements (trans-Andean) and could potentially occur in North America. Like skimmers in other parts of the world, the two South American subspecies reside primarily in rivers, making North American Black Skimmer the only skimmer population that is primarily coastal.

**PLUMAGE INFO** Appearance is not greatly affected seasonally; nonbreeding adults show a messy white band across the back of the neck, but are otherwise nearly identical to breeding adults. Fresh juveniles have a unique appearance created by broad tan fringes to the feathers of the upperparts; however, these fringes wear off quickly, exposing a dark plumage that looks like a duller version of the adults'. During their first winter, young skimmers have a distinctive blotchy appearance as they slowly acquire black mantle feathers that contrast with worn and faded juvenile feathers.

BLACK SKIMMER 3 Breeding (alt.) adults. July, FL. While skimmers have remarkably broad-based bills, the bills are laterally compressed, like the blade of a knife, to facilitate slicing through the water. The eyes are located on the sides of the head, giving the bird excellent peripheral vision but only a narrow field of binocular vision directly in front, facilitating its ability to accurately position its bill.

BLACK SKIMMER 4 Breeding (alt.) adult. April, TX. The unique bill slices the water, the upper mandible poised to snap down and grab the moment the lower touches a fish. Because the foraging style brings it so close to the water, its wingbeats do not extend below the body like those of most birds; instead, they are nearly always well above the body, creating a very distinctive appearance and giving the wingbeats an unmistakable cadence.

BLACK SKIMMER 5 Breeding (alt.) adult. July, NJ. Dustin Welch. The poster child for extreme avian adaptation. Every aspect of a Black Skimmer is honed to maximize its unique feeding style.

BLACK SKIMMER 6 Breeding (alt.) adults with Sandwich Tern, and Laughing Gull, Sanderling. April, FL. Small flocks often mix with terns and gulls while large flocks usually keep themselves separate from other birds. Note how the extraordinarily long wings merge seamlessly with the body on the front right bird, giving it a markedly attenuated appearance.

BLACK SKIMMER 7 Nonbreeding (basic) adults. Nov., GA. The size difference between the sexes in Black Skimmer can be striking, the difference in bill length and depth at the base even more so, with males being larger. The base of the bill is often orange, tinged with red, on females, and slightly washed-out orange on males, but the difference is fairly slight. The white hindneck is the only notable difference between nonbreeding and breeding plumages.

**BLACK SKIMMER 8** Recently fledged juvenile. Aug., NJ. Jesse Amesbury. The extremely broad, buffy fringes of fresh juveniles briefly create an appearance unlike any other time in the life of a skimmer. These fringes fade rapidly to gray and wear off to expose darker central parts of the feathers, so that by September, when they begin a molt to replace these feathers, their appearance is already strikingly different. It is a good example of appearance alteration not caused by molt. Also note the short wings and bill. Large bird species often fledge before all their extremities are fully grown; a particularly long bill, like that of an adult skimmer, may not reach full length for months after they fledge.

**BLACK SKIMMER 9** Juveniles and breeding (alt.) adults. Nov., NJ. Dustin Welch. Older juveniles have already worn away much of those broad, buffy feather fringes.

**BLACK SKIMMER 10** First-cycle with Royal Terns and Laughing Gull. Sept., GA. This individual retains most of its juvenile feathers, now heavily worn, and looks like a dingy version of a nonbreeding adult. It is just beginning to acquire fresh feathers on the back and scapulars, giving it a patchy appearance that continues throughout the first winter as new dark feathers are molted in, and the remaining juvenile feathers fade and look more and more tattered.

**BLACK SKIMMER 11** Immature (first-cycle). March, FL. This worn first-cycle bird shows a broad pale hindneck like an adult in winter plumage but has a grayish crown and brown-tinged back, whereas these areas would be blackish on an adult.

BLACK SKIMMER 12 Mixed ages, primarily nonbreeding (basic) adults. Nov., GA. Strikingly beautiful and distinctive, unlike terns, they sometimes fly in nearly synchronized flocks. Watching as the chaos of a flock of skimmers taking off quickly settles into order, the wingbeats and movements in perfect rhythm, even their calls reaching an orderly cadence, is one of the amazing experiences in nature.

BLACK SKIMMER 13 Breeding (alt.) adults, compared with Laughing Gull and Sandwich and Royal Terns. April, TX. Black Skimmers occasionally sit on their "heels" or fully lie down on the ground. The lying posture is often accompanied by open-billed panting and is a means of regulating temperature. Note the more reddish base of the bill on the left bird compared to the bird in the background or the right bird. This reddish color occurs more regularly in females, while a more orange base to the bill is associated with males.

**BLACK SKIMMER 14** Breeding (alt.) adults. April, TX. Flocks of skimmers feeding in unison are uncommon, but they do occur in locations with high concentrations of food. Notice how the wings seem oversized in comparison to the body. The graceful, slow-motion wingbeats on swept back wings held high above the body dominate the impression of skimmers in flight. Two of the skimmers in this image are still growing flight feathers and have pale spotting on the nape. These skimmers may be adults simultaneously completing the prebasic molt (primaries) and prealternate molt (nape), or, particularly in the case of the individual with three retained old primaries, they may be second-cycle birds.

**BLACK SKIMMER 15** Breeding (alt.) adults. July, NJ. While group feeding is somewhat unusual pairs do feed in tandem frequently, strafing a long stretch of water before turning together and cleaving the surface of the water back the way they came.

**BLACK SKIMMER 16** Breeding (alt.) adult. April, TX. Like many aerial feeders, Black Skimmers have extremely protracted molt periods. This individual in April is still in the process of replacing its primaries, a process begun the prior summer. Now only the old outermost primaries remain, their narrower tips compared to the adjacent fresh primaries projecting slightly at the point of the wing.

**BLACK SKIMMER 17** Breeding (alt.) adult. Aug., GA. Black Skimmers often sync their foraging excursions with the low tide even if the low tide occurs at night, though they are most apt to do so on moonlit nights. Their vertical pupils allow their eyes to adjust to low light conditions nearly as well as to daylight.

Answers to the quiz questions in the book are listed below in order of appearance.

1. **CASPIAN TERN 7**, p. 23 – In the far left corner is an adult Caspian Tern. The two birds immediately to the adult's right are Royal Terns, while the bird behind them and to the right is the second Caspian Tern, a first-cycle bird with dark streaking on the head in roughly the shape of the black cap of the adult and a dull orange bill with a dark tip.
2. **ROYAL TERN 14**, p. 34 – The pale gray back feathers are recently replaced, but the wing coverts, tertials, and primaries are worn feathers retained from juvenile plumage, making this a first-cycle or first-winter Caspian Tern.
3. **SANDWICH TERN 5**, p. 48 – This is a difficult challenge, and there may be no way to discern the answer with absolute certainty. Personally, I count six Common Terns and five Forster's. There are three Commons together in the upper right corner, another two in the upper center of the image, and a very out-of-focus one diagonally down and right from them, with a very dark gray belly. The only perched *Sterna* is a Forster's that is right of center, tucked behind the Laughing Gull with its neck outstretched. Another clear Forster's is far right of center, about to fly out of frame with a Black Skimmer behind it.
4. **GULL-BILLED TERN 6**, p. 65 – The bird second from the left is a juvenile Gull-billed Tern. The soft peach wash to the back is only present during juvenile plumage. Note that the posture of this bird—body angle downward, head up, mouth agape—is typical of begging juveniles.
5. **GULL-BILLED TERN 7**, p. 65 – The uniformly darkened, folded primaries and dark-centered tertials are retained juvenile feathers. This tells us that this is a worn first-cycle Forster's Tern, roughly ten months old. While precisely aging immature terns is often a fraught task, birds retaining juvenile feathers give us a solid starting point to make definitive statements about their age.
6. **ROSEATE TERN 11**, p. 111 – The adult is a Roseate Tern. The diagnostic white trailing edge to the primaries is visible, as are the brilliant red legs that are significantly brighter than the dull red base to the bill. Also note the extensive black tip to the bill that extends farther back on the lower mandible.
7. **ROSEATE TERN 13**, p. 112 – From back left: juvenile Common, adult Common (front left), adult Roseate (obscured), juvenile Roseate, adult Roseate, and juvenile Roseate. The juvenile Common can be identified by the orange base to the lower mandible (juvenile Roseates have all-black bills), the shape of the black hood (this also eliminates juvenile Arctic Tern), and the stronger shoulder bar. The adult Common can be identified by its matte gray color, molt limit in the dead center of the folded primaries, and dingy red legs and base to the bill. The obscured adult Roseate can be identified by its very pale color and by the color of the base of the bill. Both juvenile Roseates are easily identified by their all-black bills, their extensive dark hoods and mottled foreheads, the V-shaped rather than U-shaped dark markings to the scapular and tertial feathers, and the white trailing edges to the folded primaries. The adult Roseate left of center is a classic late-summer Roseate.
8. ***STERNA* TERN 11**, p. 121 – The bird in the top right corner of the image is an out-of-focus Common Tern. Immediately below that Common Tern is the bird we are looking for, an adult Roseate Tern. It has an entirely black bill and more limited black in the outer primaries than a Common Tern.
9. ***STERNA* TERN 14**, p. 123 – While this image is a challenge, it is also littered with immature Arctic Terns. Perhaps the easiest to find is the first-summer type at the bottom center of the frame with the tip of its right wing cropped off. From there, diagonally up and left is a subadult Arctic with dark gray plumage, a very dark red bill, and limited white on the underwing. The rest of the Arctics in the image are first-summer types. From the original Arctic at the bottom of the image, go to the right, and you will notice a Common Tern with a blurry right wing; immediately above that blurry wing is a group of four terns in the background. The lead bird is most likely an Arctic, as are possibly some of the three immediately behind it, but we aren't counting these. From the blurry-winged Common Tern, the bird directly above, to the right of the background group of four, with its wings raised, is another Arctic, with its wings raised. The tip of this bird's left wing is touching the vent of another Arctic in the background, and the bird immediately behind, with its tail chopped out of frame, is another Arctic. At the top right is a tight knot of terns, and the bird at the bottom right of this knot is another Arctic. At the center of the left third of the frame is another obvious Arctic with one wing up and one down. Immediately above that, there is a tight knot of birds, and the topmost bird on the left-hand side of the image is another Arctic. The final Arctic is at the far left center with its bill chopped off and its wingtip raised above the waterline in the background.

Alderfer, J., ed. 2006. *Complete Birds of North America.* Washington, DC: National Geographic Society.

Alderfer, J., and J. L. Dunn. 2007. *Birding Essentials.* Washington, DC: National Geographic Society.

Alerstam, T., J. Bäckman, J. Grönroos, P. Olofsson, and R. Strandberg. 2019. Hypotheses and tracking results about the longest migration: the case of the arctic tern. *Ecology and Evolution* 9(17):9511–9531.

Andrews, R., and R. Righter. 1992. *Colorado Birds.* Denver, CO: Denver Museum of Natural History.

Armistead, G. L., and B. L. Sullivan. 2016. *Better Birding: Tips, Tools, and Concepts for the Field.* Princeton, NJ: Princeton University Press.

Arnold, J. M., S. A. Oswald, I.C.T. Nisbet, P. Pyle, and M. A. Patten. 2020. Common Tern (*Sterna hirundo*), version 1.0. In *Birds of the World*, ed. S. M. Billerman. Ithaca, NY: Cornell Lab of Ornithology.

Beaman, M., and S. Madge. 1998. *The Handbook of Bird Identification for Europe and the Western Palearctic.* London, UK: Christopher Helm.

Behrens, K., and C. Cox. 2013. *Seawatching: Eastern Waterbirds in Flight.* Peterson Reference Guide Series. Boston: Houghton Mifflin Harcourt.

Blomdahl, A., B. Breife, and N. Holmström. 2003. *Flight Identification of European Seabirds.* London, UK: Christopher Helm.

Bridge, E. S., and I. C. Nisbet. 2004. Wing molt and assortative mating in Common Terns: a test of the molt-signaling hypothesis. *The Condor* 106(2):336–343.

Bridge, E. S., G. Voelker, C. W. Thompson, A. W. Jones, and A. J. Baker. 2007. Effects of size and migratory behavior on the evolution of wing molt in terns (*Sternae*): a phylogenetic comparative study. *Auk* 124:841–856.

Brinkley, E. 2010. A White-winged Tern at Chincoteague National Wildlife Refuge in 2002, with comments on identification and ageing of the species and a review of regional records. *Raven* 81:3–10.

Buckley, P. A., and F. G. Buckley. 1984. Cayenne Tern new to North America with comments on its relationship to Sandwich Tern. *Auk* 101:396–398.

Buckley, P. A., F. G. Buckley, and S. G. Mlodinow. 2021. Royal Tern (*Thalasseus maximus*), version 1.1. In *Birds of the World*, ed. S. M. Billerman. Ithaca, NY: Cornell Lab of Ornithology.

Burness, G. P., K. L. Lefevre, and C. T. Collins. 2020. Elegant Tern (*Thalasseus elegans*), version 1.0. In *Birds of the World*, eds. A. F. Poole and F. B. Gill. Ithaca, NY: Cornell Lab of Ornithology.

Cabot, D., and I. Nisbet. 2013. *Terns.* London, UK: HarperCollins Publishers.

Chardine, J. W., R. D. Morris, M. Gochfeld, J. Burger, G. M. Kirwan, and E.F.J. Garcia. 2020. Brown Noddy (*Anous stolidus*), version 1.0. In *Birds of the World*, ed. S. M. Billerman. Ithaca, NY: Cornell Lab of Ornithology.

Collins, C. T. 1997. Hybridization of a Sandwich and an Elegant Tern in California. *Western Birds* 28:169–173.

Cormons, G. D. 1976. Roseate Tern bill color change in relation to nesting status and food supply. *The Wilson Bulletin* 88(3):377–528.

Craik, J.C.A. 1994. Aspects of wing moult in Common Tern *Sterna hirundo*. *Ringing & Migration* 15(1):27–32.

Cuthbert, F. J., and L. R. Wires. 2020. Caspian Tern (*Hydropogne caspia*), version 1.0. In *Birds of the World*, ed. S. M. Billerman. Ithaca, NY: Cornell Lab of Ornithology.

Dixey, A. E., A. Ferguson, R. Heywood, and A. R. Taylor. 1981. Aleutian Tern: new to the western Palearctic. *British Birds* 74:411–416.

Donaldson, G. 1968. Bill color changes in adult Roseate Terns. *The Auk* 85(4):662–668.

Donaldson, G., and H. Hayes. 1969. Roseate Tern in unusual plumage. *Bird-Banding* 40(3):255.

Dufour, P., J. Gernigon, and P. A. Crochet. 2021. Identification and occurrence of hybrids Elegant x Sandwich Tern in Europe. *Dutch Birding* 43:249–256.

Dufour, P., J. Jones, and P. A. Crochet. 2016. Occurrence of multiple Elegant Terns confirmed in Western Europe. *Birdguides* http://www.birdguides.com/articles/occurrence-of-multiple-elegant-terns-confirmed-in-western-europe.

Dufour P., J.-M. Pons, J. M. Collinson, J. Gernigon, J. I. Dies, P. Sourrouille, and P.-A. Crochet. 2016. Multilocus barcoding confirms the occurrence of Elegant Terns in Western Europe. *Journal of Ornithology* 158(2):351–361.

Dunn, J. L., and J. Alderfer. 2017. *National Geographic Field Guide to the Birds of North America.* 7th ed. Washington, DC: National Geographic Society.

Efe, M. A., E. S. Tavares, A. J. Baker, and S. L. Bonatto. 2009. Multigene phylogeny and DNA barcoding indicate that the Sandwich Tern complex (*Thalasseus sandvicensis, Laridae, Sternini*) comprises two species. *Molecular Phylogenetic Evolution* 52:263–267.

Garner, M., I. Lewington, and J. Crook. 2007. Identification of American Sandwich Tern. *Dutch Birding* 29:273–287.

Gauger, V. H. 2020. Black Noddy (*Anous minutus*), version 1.0. In *Birds of the World*, ed. S. M. Billerman. Ithaca, NY: Cornell Lab of Ornithology.

Gochfeld, M., and J. Burger. 2020. Roseate Tern (*Sterna dougallii*), version 1.0. In *Birds of the World*, ed. S. M. Billerman. Ithaca, NY: Cornell Lab of Ornithology.

Gochfeld, M., J. Burger, D. A. Christie, G. M. Kirwan, and E.F.J. Garcia. 2020. White-winged Tern (*Chlidonias leucopterus*), version 1.0. In *Birds of the World*, eds. J. del Hoyo, A. Elliot, J. Sargatal, D. A. Christie, and E. de Juana. Ithaca, NY: Cornell Lab of Ornithology.

Gochfeld, M., J. Burger, G. M. Kirwan, and E.F.J. Garcia. 2020. Whiskered Tern (*Chlidonias hybrida*), version 1.0. In *Birds of the World*, eds. J. del Hoyo, A. Elliot, J. Sargatal, D. A. Christie, and E. de Juana. Ithaca, NY: Cornell Lab of Ornithology.

Gochfeld, M., J. Burger, and K. L. Lefevre. 2020. Black Skimmer (*Rynchops niger*), version 1.0. In *Birds of the World*, ed. S. M. Billerman. Ithaca, NY: Cornell Lab of Ornithology.

Grant, P. J., and R. E. Scott. 1969. Field identification of juvenile Common, Arctic and Roseate Terns. *British Birds* 62(8):297–300.

Grant, P. J., R. E. Scott, and D.I.M. Wallace. 1971. Further notes on the 'portlandica' plumage phase of terns. *British Birds* 64:19–22.

Greenlaw, J. S., B. Pranty, and R. Bowman. 2014. The Robertson and Woolfenden Florida bird species: An annotated list. *Florida Ornithological Society* Special Publication 8:1–435.

Grimes, L. G. 1974. A radar study of tern movements along the coast of Ghana. *Ibis* 119(1):28–36.

Hall, J. A. 1998. Vocal repertoire of Forster's Tern. *Colonial Waterbirds* 21(3):388–405.

Hamilton, R. A., M. A. Patten, and R. A. Erickson, eds. 2007. *Rare Birds of California.* Camarillo, CA: Western Field Ornithologists.

Haney, J. C., D. S. Lee, and R. D. Morris. 2020. Bridled Tern (*Onychoprion anaethetus*), version 1.0. In *Birds of the World*, ed. S. M. Billerman. Ithaca, NY: Cornell Lab of Ornithology.

Hatch, J. J., M. Gochfeld, J. Burger, and E.F.J. Garcia. 2020. Arctic Tern (*Sterna paradisaea*), version 1.0. In *Birds of the World*, ed. S. M. Billerman. Ithaca, NY: Cornell Lab of Ornithology.

Hayes, F. E. 2004. Variability and interbreeding of Sandwich Terns and Cayenne Terns in the Virgin Islands, with comments on their systematic relationship. *North American Birds* 57:566–572.

Hays, H. 1971. Roseate Tern, *Sterna dougallii*, banded on the Atlantic Coast recovered on Pacific. *Bird-Banding* 42(4): 295.

——. 1975. Probable Common x Roseate Tern hybrids. *The Auk* 92(2):219–234.

Hays, H., J. Hudon, G. Cormons, J. Dicostanzo, and P. Lima. 2006. The pink feather blush of the Roseate Tern. *Waterbirds: The International Journal of Waterbird Biology* 29(3):296–301.

Heath, S. R., E. H. Dunn, and D. J. Argo. 2020. Black Tern (*Chlidonias niger*), version 1.0. In *Birds of the World*, ed. S. M. Billerman. Ithaca, NY: Cornell Lab of Ornithology.

Hess, G. K., R. L. West, M. V. Barnhill III, and L. M. Fleming. 2000. *Birds of Delaware.* Pittsburgh, PA: University of Pittsburgh Press.

Hill, N. P., and K. D. Bishop. 1999. Possible winter quarters of the Aleutian Tern? *Wilson Bulletin* 111(4):559–560.

Howell, S.N.G. 2010. *Molt in North American Birds.* Peterson Reference Guide Series. Boston: Houghton Mifflin Harcourt.

Howell, S.N.G., C. Corben, P. Pyle, and D. I. Rogers. 2003. The first basic problem: a review of molt and plumage homologies. *The Condor* 105(4):635–653.

Howell, S.N.G., I. Lewington, and W. Russell. 2014. *Rare Birds of North America.* Princeton, NJ: Princeton University Press.

Howell, S.N.G., and B. L. Sullivan. 2018. *Peterson Guide to Bird Identification in 12 Steps.* Boston: Houghton Mifflin Harcourt.

Howell, S.N.G., and K. Zufelt. 2019. *Oceanic Birds of the World: A Photo Guide.* Princeton, NJ: Princeton University Press.

Hume, R., R. Still, A. Swash, and H. Harrop. 2021. *Europe's Birds: An Identification Guide.* Princeton, NJ: Princeton University Press.

Hume, R. A. 1993. Common, Arctic and Roseate Terns: an identification review. *British Birds* 86:2010–2017.

Humphrey, P. S., and K. C. Parkes. 1959. An approach to the study of molts and plumages. *The Auk* 76(1):1–31.

Lewington, I., P. Alström, and P. Colston. 1991. *A Field Guide to the Rare Birds of Britain and Europe.* London, UK: HarperCollins.

Martin, G. R., R. McNeil, and L. M. Rojas. 2007. Vision and foraging technique of skimmers (*Rynchopidae*). *Ibis* 149(4):750–757.

McCarthy, E. M. 2006. *Handbook of Avian Hybrids of the World.* New York: Oxford University Press.

McNicholl, M. K., P. E. Lowther, and J. A. Hall. 2020. Forster's Tern (*Sterna forsteri*), version 1.0. In *Birds of the World*, eds. A. F. Poole and F. B. Gill. Ithaca, NY: Cornell Lab of Ornithology.

Mitra, S. S., and P. A. Buckley. 2000. Cayenne Tern on Long Island, New York: North America's fourth. *Kingbird* 50:358–367.

Molina, K. C., J. F. Parnell, R. M. Erwin, J. del Hoyo, N. Collar, G. M. Kirwan, and E.F. J. Garcia. 2020. Gull-billed Tern (*Gelochelidon nilotica*), version 1.0. In *Birds of the World*, ed. S. M. Billerman. Ithaca, NY: Cornell Lab of Ornithology.

Monticelli, D., and J. A. Ramos. 2007. Plumage characteristics and return rate of one-year-old tropical Roseate Terns. *Waterbirds: The International Journal of Waterbird Biology* 30(1):58–63.

Mullarney, K., L. Svensson, D. Zetterström, and P. J. Grant. 2000. *The Complete Guide to the Birds of Europe*. Princeton, NJ: Princeton University Press.

Nisbet, I.C.T., and N. Ratcliffe. 2008. Comparative demographics of tropical and temperate Roseate Terns. *Waterbirds* 31(3):346–356.

North, M. R. 2020. Aleutian Tern (*Onychoprion aleuticus*), version 1.0. In *Birds of the World*, ed. S. M. Billerman. Ithaca, NY: Cornell Lab of Ornithology.

Norton, R. L. 1984. Cayenne x Sandwich Terns nesting in Virgin Islands, Greater Antilles. *Journal of Field* Ornithology 1984:243–246.

O'Brien, M., R. Crossley, and K. Karlson. 2006. The Shorebird Guide. Boston: Houghton Mifflin Harcourt.

Oehlers, S., N. Catterson, M. Goldstein, and S. Pyare. 2010. Aleutian Terns: a migration mystery. *SourDough Notes* https://www.fs.usda.gov/Internet/FSE_DOCUMENTS/stelprdb5275100.pdf.

Olsen, K. M., and H. Larsson. 1995. Terns of Europe and North America. Princeton, NJ: Princeton University Press.

Palestis, B. G., I.C.T. Nisbet, J. J. Hatch, P. Szczys, and J. A. Spendelow. 2012. Morphometric sexing of northwest Atlantic Roseate Terns. *Waterbirds* 35(3):479–484.

Paul, R. T., B. Pranty, A. F. Paul, A. B. Hodgson, and D. J. Powell. 2003. Probable hybridization between an Elegant Tern and Sandwich Tern in West Central Florida: the first confirmed North American breeding record away from the Pacific Coast. *North American Birds* 57:280–282.

Peacock, F. 2017. Identifying Southern Africa's terns. *Faansie Peacock Blog* https://faansiepeacock.com/identifying-antarctic-terns.

Pyle, P. 2008. *Identification Guide to North American Birds: Part 2*. Bolinas, CA: Slate Creek Press.

Robertson, W. B., D. R. Paulson, and C. R. Mason. 1964. A tern new to the United States. *The Auk* 78(3):423–425.

Rowlett, R. A. 1980. Observations of marine birds and mammals in the northern Chesapeake Bight. U.S. Fish and Wildlife Service.

Schreiber, E. A., C. J. Feare, B. A. Harrington, B. G. Murray Jr., W. B. Robertson Jr., and G. E. Woolfenden. 2020. Sooty Tern (*Onychoprion fuscatus*), version 1.0. In *Birds of the World*, ed. S. M. Billerman. Ithaca, NY: Cornell Lab of Ornithology.

Shealer, D., J. S. Liechty, A. R. Pierce, P. Pyle, and M. A. Patten. 2020. Sandwich Tern (*Thalasseus sandvicensis*), version 1.0. In *Birds of the World*, ed. S. M. Billerman. Ithaca, NY: Cornell Lab of Ornithology.

Shoch, D. T., and S. N. Howell. 2013. Occurrence and identification of vagrant "orange-billed terns" in eastern North America. *North American Birds* 67:188–209.

Sibley, D. A. 2002. *Sibley's Birding Basics*. New York: Alfred A. Knopf.

——. 2014. *The Sibley Guide to Birds*. 2nd ed. New York: Alfred A. Knopf.

Spendelow, J. A. 2015. First record of a banded Sandwich Tern (*Thalasseus sandvicensis*) moving from England to the United States. *Waterbirds* 38(4):425–426.

Stoddart, A. 2016. Common, Arctic, and Roseate Terns photo ID guide. *Birdwatch* https://www.birdguides.com/articles/identification/common-arctic-and-roseate-terns-photo-id-guide.

——. 2017. Marsh tern photo ID guide. *Birdwatch* https://www.birdguides.com/articles/identification/marsh-tern-photo-id-guide.

Strange, M. 2000. *A Photographic Guide to the Birds of Southeast Asia: Including the Philippines and Borneo*. Princeton, NJ: Princeton University Press.

Thompson, B. C., J. A. Jackson, J. Burger, L. A. Hill, E. M. Kirsch, and J. L. Atwood. 2020. Least Tern (*Sternula antillarum*), version 1.0. In *Birds of the World*, eds. A. F. Poole and F. B. Gill. Ithaca, NY: Cornell Lab of Ornithology.

Thompson, B. C., and R. D. Slack. 1983. Molt-breeding overlap and timing of pre-basic molt in Texas Least Terns. *Journal of Field Ornithology* 54(2):187–190.

Toochin, R., P. Hamel, and M. Hearne. 2017. Status and occurrence of Aleutian Tern (*Onychoprion aleuticus*) in British Columbia. *E-Fauna BC* https://ibis.geog.ubc.ca/biodiversity/efauna/documents/ALTE-article-RT-PH-MH.pdf.

Velarde, E., and P. Rojo. 2012. Presumed hybrid Elegant x Cabot's Terns *Thalasseus elegans* x *T. acuflavida* in Isla Rasa, Gulf of California, Mexico. *Marine Ornithology* 40:25–29.

Vinicombe, K. E. 1989. Field identification of Gull-billed Tern. *British Birds* 82:3–13.

Voelker, G. 1996. A hypothesis for seasonal color change in the genus *Sterna*. *Journal of Avian Biology* 27(3):257–259.

——. 1997. The molt cycle of Arctic Tern, with comments on aging criteria (El ciclo de muda de *Sterna paradisaea* y comentarios sobre los criteros para asignar edades). *Journal of Field Ornithology* 68(3):400–412.

Wahl, T. R., B. Tweit, and S. G. Mlodinow, eds. 2005. *Birds of Washington: Status and Distribution.* Corvallis, OR: Oregon State University Press.

Walsh, J., V. Elia, R. Kane, and T. Halliwell. 1999. *Birds of New Jersey.* Cape May Point, NJ: New Jersey Audubon Society.

White, S. J., and C. V. Kehoe. 2001. Difficulties in determining the age of Common Terns in the field. *British Birds* 94:268–277.

Whittam, R. M. 1998. Interbreeding of Roseate and Arctic Terns. *The Wilson Bulletin* 110(1):65–70.

Wilds, C. 1993. The identification and aging of Forster's and Common Terns. *Birding* 25:94–108.